GWR THEN & NOW

GWR THEN & NOW

LAURENCE WATERS

Ian Allan Publishing

First published 1994

ISBN 0 7110 2267 4

© Ian Allan Ltd 1994

Designed by Alan C. Butcher

Published by Ian Allan Publishing

an imprint of Ian Allan Ltd, Terminal House, Station Approach, Shepperton, Surrey TW17 8AS; and printed by Ian Allan Printing Ltd, Coombelands House, Coombelands Lane, Addlestone, Weybridge, Surrey KT15 1HY.

Reprinted 2007

Page 1
Bedminster
'County' class 4-6-0 No 1016 *County of Hants* passes through Bedminster in the 1950s with a through service from Plymouth to Glasgow. The station at Bedminster is still open but the platforms are obscured as an HST passes through on 28 November 1993 with an up service from Weston-super-Mare to Paddington. Bedminster signalbox was closed on 6 April 1970. The most extraordinary change is undoubtedly in the skyline of Bristol.
G. Herion/Steven Park

Pages 2 and 3
Saunderton
An ex-Great Western '9400' class 0-6-0PT hauls a mixed goods through the small station at Saunderton in July 1961. Depending on the load the engine is probably working hard as the station was situated on the stiff climb up through the Chilterns between High Wycombe and Princes Risborough. The signalbox here closed on 16 November 1975. The down-side buildings have now been removed but the up-side waiting room still survives as two-car Turbo unit No 165019 arrives with the 12.10pm service from Marylebone to Princes Risborough 19 June 1993. The large engineering works seen on both pictures has now ceased trading, a victim of the recession.
C. R. L. Coles/Author

Below and right:
Boncath
One of the intermediate stations on the Cardigan branch was at Boncath. The station is seen here on 28 August 1956 as '4500' class 2-6-2T No 4550 arrives with the 11.35am service from Whitland. The station was closed with the branch on 27 May 1963 and lay derelict for a number of years before being sold. In this shot taken on 26 September 1993 the trackbed has been swallowed up in the undergrowth, but the platform face can still be seen under the accumulating rubbish.
G. F. Bannister/Geoff Wright

Contents

Introduction

The Great Western Railway Co was inaugurated in 1835 to construct a railway between London and Bristol. The first section of the line from Paddington to Maidenhead was opened on 4 June 1838. Passenger services between London and Bristol commenced just two years later on 30 June 1841. Gradually the main line system was extended. In the southwest, services between Paddington and Exeter via Bristol commenced in May 1844; they were extended through to Plymouth in May 1848 and, with the opening of the Royal Albert Bridge, to Penzance in May 1859.

South Wales was reached in 1851, services running via Swindon, Gloucester and Chepstow. The first section of what was to become the South Wales main line had been opened between Swindon and Gloucester in May 1845. In September 1851 the line was extended from Gloucester through to Grange Court and Chepstow. Here it connected with the South Wales Railway which had opened its own line between Landore and Chepstow in June 1850. Gradually the line was extended westwards and in April 1856 through services were inaugurated between Paddington and New

Milford (Neyland), which for a number of years was the terminus of the line. The third major route, to Birmingham and beyond, began to take shape with the opening of the Oxford Railway between Didcot junction and Oxford in June 1844. The line was extended through to Birmingham in October 1852 and to Wolverhampton in November 1854.

Main line services to South Wales, the southwest and Birmingham were speeded up with the opening of three new 'cut-off' lines in 1903, 1906 and 1910 respectively. The first of these from Wootton Bassett to Patchway opened in May 1903.

This new direct route was made possible with the opening of the Severn Tunnel in December 1886. The second of the new 'cut off' routes, to the southwest, from Patney to Cogload junction was opened in April 1906. The final 'cut off' route, from Ashendon junction to Aynho, was completed in April 1910.

The Grouping in 1923 saw the Great Western absorb a total of 32 independent companies which resulted in its route mileage climbing from its pre-Grouping level of 3,026 up to 3,804. The total mileage of all tracks (including sidings) operated by the Great Western rose almost overnight from 6,645 to 8,993, a far cry from its 1838 total of just 24 miles. From those humble beginnings the Great Western had grown to become one of the largest and most well-known railway companies in the world. This was helped by the fact that, after the Grouping, the Great Western

was the only major company to retain its identity. It is also worth noting that in 1838 the company owned just 19 locomotives, yet by 1947, the last year of the company's existence, this figure had risen to nearly 4,000.

Nationalisation in 1948 made little difference to the company both in size and operation. But, with the modernisation programme of the 1950s and early 1960s also came the closure of a considerable number of secondary routes and branch lines. The overall route mileage was reduced further when in 1963 regional boundary changes saw almost all of the old system in the West Midlands, the Borders, and North Wales transferred to the London Midland Region. This loss was partially counterbalanced by the transfer of part of the ex-LSWR system in Devon and Cornwall to Western Region control. This did not last for long, for within a few years the Western Region

had closed many of the ex-LSWR lines.

By 1985, the 150th anniversary of the old company, the Western Region was operating services over approximately 1,900 route-miles, of which about 400 were for freight only. Since 10 June 1986 passenger and freight services have been sectorised; and from 1 April 1994 effectively de-nationalised as a prelude to privatisation. All main line services to Wales, the West of England and the Midlands are operated by InterCity. Intermediate services over the rest of the system are operated by the Regional Railways sector with the exception of the Thames & Chiltern and West Midlands areas which are operated by Network SouthEast and Centro respectively. Freight traffic has also been split into Railfreight Coal, Petroleum and Construction, all of which operate over the area covered. Today the system is at

Henley-in-Arden
Henley-in-Arden was originally served by a short branch from the GW main line at Rowington. The original terminus station at Henley was closed to passengers on 1 July 1908 (it remained open for goods until 5 November 1962). For the opening of the North Warwickshire line on 1 December 1907 a new station was constructed at Henley-in-Arden. It is seen here in March 1957 as 2-6-2T No 3101 arrives with a service from Moor Street. Apart from the removal of the buildings on the island platform, little has changed as Sprinter No 150013 arrives with the 10.22am service from Birmingham Snow Hill to Stratford on 27 November 1993.
Real Photos/Author

the crossroads; privatisation may result in a revival for many lines, but sadly it might also mean closure for others.

To produce a 'Then and Now' book which covers every station or junction on what was the old Great Western system would be a mammoth task and would run into several volumes. Therefore in order to cover the system in a single volume it has been necessary to select locations that give an overall impression of just what remains. I have divided the book into five regional areas and concentrated on the existing railway network, but to make matters more interesting I have also included a number of sites where the railway has gone for ever. As will soon be apparent from the following pages, motive power these days comprises mainly HSTs and Classes 143, 150, 153, 158, 165 and 166 units. Locomotive-hauled services are now at a premium with Classes 37, 47, 56 and 60 providing the bulk of the motive power. Therefore in order to avoid constant repetition and to show details of what does or does not remain, I have deliberately avoided including a train in every picture. At some locations the sparsity of ser-

vices makes this a very easy task!

It has certainly been an interesting exercise travelling around the country to some locations that I have not visited for over 30 years; clutching a 'Then' picture in one hand, and a camera in the other. At many locations the change has been remarkable, whilst at others there has been hardly any change at all. At many locations it is not now possible to re-shoot the scene without trespassing on to the railway or privately-owned land. At these locations permission has almost always been forthcoming; but, on the few occasions when it has been refused it has been necessary to re-shoot the scene from a slightly different angle. There was also the problem of over-grown foliage, the obvious answer is always to carry a chainsaw, but from the environmental point of view this is not a good idea. So once again in these circumstances a different angle has been used.

To try and make the book as up to date as possible many of the 'Now' pictures were taken between August 1993 and January 1994. Unfortunately this has coincided with one of the wettest winters for some years and has made choosing

the right days to shoot difficult. In order to produce the book within this time-scale it has been necessary to call upon the assistance of several other photographers who have kindly re-shot a number of locations that the author has not had time to reach. I would therefore like to thank the following for their kind assistance: Dane Garrod, Briane Davies, Geoff Wright, Peter Heath, Amyas Crump, Alan Cornish, Michael Baker, Clive Turner, Peter Triggs, Barrie Fenton and Stephen Park.

I would also like to thank the following for supplying many of the 'Then' pictures, J. D. Edwards, R. C. Riley, Michael Mensing, Brian Morrison, Dr Geoff Smith, Steve Boorne, J. F. Loader, Hugh Ballantyne, D. Trevor Rowe, the Ian Allan Library and The Great Western Trust. Much of the background information regarding opening and closing dates etc has been obtained from the Great Western Trust Historic Archive at Didcot Railway Centre.

Special thanks to Chris Potts for signalling information and to Glenys Davies and Peter Webber for checking the manuscript.

Laurence Waters
Oxford 1994

A selection of GWR publicity posters from the GW Trust's collection.

8

Section 1
Thames and Chiltern

Middlesex, Berkshire, Bucks and Oxon

The Thames and Chiltern area in this book covers many of the extant or former lines and branches that are situated between Paddington, Didcot, Oxford and Banbury.

The widespread closures of the 1960s probably affected this area less than most. The Great Western main line out of Paddington is of course still intact and is probably as busy as ever. The cut-off route to Banbury, opened by the Great Western in 1910, was downgraded from main line status during the late 1960s, with the section between Princes Risborough and Aynho junction being singled in November 1968. In recent years the 'Chiltern Line' as it is now known has been the subject of considerable investment with a corresponding upturn in passenger numbers. Of the many branch lines in the area, those to Blenheim & Woodstock (closed to passengers 1 March 1954), Fairford (18 June 1962), Uxbridge Vine Street (10 September 1962) and Abingdon (9 September 1963) unfortunately have gone for ever. The Didcot, Newbury & Southampton Railway, once a major through route was closed to passengers on 10 September 1962, and is also now but a memory. All of the others are still operational, albeit some only in part. Passenger services still operate to Windsor, Henley, Marlow and Aylesbury whilst sections of the Brentford and Staines branches remain open for freight traffic.

For the steam enthusiast, sections of the Watlington branch (closed to passengers 1957) and the Wallingford branch (closed to passengers 1959) are now being operated by railway preservation societies. The old Great Western steam depots at Southall and Didcot are now operated as

steam centres. The depot at Southall, which was closed by BR in 1986, is still in its infancy but at Didcot the Great Western Society has been in occupation since 1966 and has established what is arguably the best collection of ex-Great Western artefacts in the country.

Main line passenger services to and from Paddington are operated by the InterCity sector. 'Thames Line' intermediate services to Oxford and Newbury are operated by Network South-East who also operate the 'Chiltern Line' services between Marylebone, Princes Risborough, Aylesbury and Banbury.

In recent years the number of locomotive-hauled passenger trains in the Thames and Chiltern area has been reduced considerably with only the InterCity cross country trains to the south coast via Oxford and Reading and the through services between Paddington and the northwest still being operated by the ubiquitous Class 47s.

InterCity main line services to the southwest, Bristol, Swansea and Cheltenham are operated using HST sets. From the start of the winter 1993 timetable the Bristol and South Wales services have been designated 'InterCity Shuttles' with a half-hourly interval service to Bristol

and an hourly interval service to Swansea. Since October 1993 all Network SouthEast Thames & Chiltern Line services have been operated using Class 165 and 166 Turbo units. This has resulted in the closure of Old Oak Common and Marylebone DMU depots. Servicing of Thames Line units is now undertaken at Reading, with Chiltern Line units being maintained at Aylesbury. A small servicing and cleaning point has recently been opened at Oxford.

The introduction of the new units has completed a multi-million pound modernisation programme for the Thames and Chiltern lines which has seen many of the remaining stations either rebuilt or refurbished. On the Chiltern Line a new station at Haddenham & Thame Parkway was opened during 1989 to serve the Thame catchment area. On the Thames Line, Paddington, Didcot and Reading have all been extensively refurbished. At Oxford the upside buildings have been demolished and replaced by a new building more in keeping with its importance as a rail centre.

Freight services in the Thames and Chiltern area are operated using Classes 37, 47, 56, 58, 59 and 60 and comprise mainly household waste, coal, oil and stone. The international Railfreight depot at Morris Cowley, which is situated on the remains of the old Oxford-Princes Risborough branch, also deals with motor vehicles and general merchandise. During 1993 Old Oak Common was reduced to a refuelling and stabling point with the closure of the locomotive works. A new stabling point for Railfreight Construction locomotives has been established at Acton and, at the time of writing, a new fuelling point for Railfreight locomotives is being constructed at Didcot.

GOLF GWR COURSES

Paddington

We start our tour of the Great Western at Brunel's masterpiece, Paddington. The present station was opened on 29 May 1854 and apart from some additional platforms and cosmetic changes still looks very much as built. A view of platform 1 from the 'Lawn' at Paddington in June 1935 as passengers prepare to board the Cornish Riviera Limited, the 10.30am service to Penzance. The '5700' class 0-6-0PT on pilot duty is No 5745. Notice the various kiosks and also the famous clock. In November 1968 the Lawn area at Paddington was extended westwards by about 37 metres and in the last few years the station has undergone a considerable amount of refurbishment. The result can partially be seen in this view taken on 20 November 1993. The roof work is as yet unfinished, and the scaffolding unfortunately obscures the clock which is still *in situ* and will itself be restored. The beautifully restored ticket offices are on the left and on the right is the new information centre.
GW Trust/Author

Paddington

The down 'Bristolian', the 8.45am Paddington-Bristol service, waits to leave platform 3 at Paddington on 20 August 1957 behind 'Castle' No 5065 *Newport Castle*. On the right an unidentified member of the class waits with the 8.50am service to Weston-super-Mare.

  This is one location where the only real change is the motive power. On 20 November 1993 a pair of HSTs occupy platforms 2 and 3 on the newly-introduced InterCity 'Shuttle' services to Bristol and South Wales.

J. D. Edwards/Author

Ranelagh Bridge Yard

A view of the locomotive servicing facility at Ranelagh Bridge Yard on 6 August 1960 with (from left to right) 'County' class No 1027 *County of Stafford*, 'Britannia' No 70025 *Western Star*, 'Castles' Nos 7003 *Elmley Castle*, 7020 *Gloucester Castle* and 5044 *Earl of Dunraven* and on the right 'King' No 6011 *King James I*. The yard was opened on 27 June 1907 and was closed to steam in April 1964. For a number of years after the withdrawal of steam traction the yard was used for servicing diesels but with the introduction of HSTs it was finally closed in 1980. As can be seen from the second photograph, the area today is used as a staff car park with 'Castles' and 'Kings' being replaced by Fords and Vauxhalls.
R C Riley/Author

Royal Oak

'1500' class 0-6-0PT No 1500 passes Royal Oak station with empty stock from Old Oak to Paddington on 30 June 1959. Royal Oak was opened by the Great Western on 30 October 1871 but is today served only by Hammersmith & City Line services. It is pictured here on 20 November 1993 as Class 165 No 165128 passes with a Thames Line stopping service from Reading. Notice the lowered track in the foreground in preparation for the forthcoming electrification work. The only other major change is the Westway which runs adjacent to the line at this point.
R. C. Riley /Author

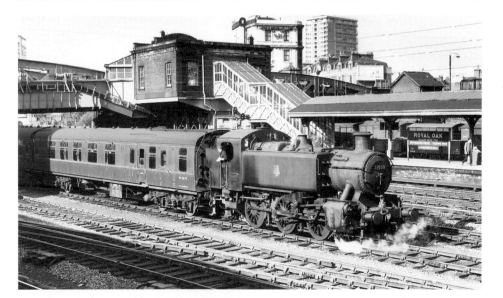

West Ealing

West Ealing station seen here on 5 August 1962. The station was opened as Castle Hill on 1 March 1871 but was renamed West Ealing on 1 July 1899. The up relief platform was staggered and can just be seen on the left under the bridge. Notice on the left the girder structure of the office building seen in the second picture.

During 1991 a new up relief platform was constructed and can be seen in this picture of Turbo No 165119 on a Greenford-Paddington service. The down main platform has now been removed and the up main fenced off.
M. Hale/Author

West Ealing junction

'Castle' class No 5037 *Monmouth Castle* heads the down 'Cathedrals Express' Paddington-Hereford service past West Ealing junction in the summer of 1959. In the background is West Ealing Junction box behind which is the milk dock. Also in view is a milk train hauled by a '5700' class 0-6-0PT.

The modern equivalent of the 'Cathedrals Express', the 'Cotswold & Malvern Express' HST service to Great Malvern, speeds through West Ealing on 20 November 1993. The signalbox closed on 13 May 1968, as did the old West Yard. The milk dock closed in 1971 but as can be seen is still *in situ*.
A. A. Sellman/Author

Hanwell

A station was opened by the Great Western at Hanwell & Elthorne on 1 December 1838 just six months after the opening of the line from Paddington (old station) to Maidenhead (Dumb Bell Bridge). The station seen here on 5 August 1960 was constructed during the quadrupling of the track in 1877. It stands on a steep embankment and is entered via a subway.

The same view on 20 November 1993 shows that the down main platform has now been removed but the remainder of the station has been tastefully restored. A feature of the up relief platform is a wonderful ex-Great Western cast iron 'Subway' sign. The gas lamps however are replicas.
M. Hale/Author

Southall

Looking down from the footbridge to the east of Southall, as 'Castle' class No 7024 *Powis Castle* passes through with an empty milk train. Behind the 'Castle' is the east end goods shed. On the right is the large locomotive depot and water softening plant.

The locomotive depot was closed in November 1986; it had closed to steam in December 1965 and was thereafter used as a DMU depot. Today it is operated as the Southall Railway Centre. The goods shed on the left was closed to rail traffic in 1973. On the far right is the remains of the Brentford branch, which was closed to passengers in 1942 but is still open for waste and aggregate traffic.
C. R. L. Coles/Author

Southall

This general view of Southall station was taken in the 1950s and shows an unidentified 'Castle' speeding through with the 7.15am service from Plymouth to Paddington. Southall was the junction station for the Brentford branch which is just out of shot on the left.

A slightly wider view on 20 November 1993 shows a pair of Turbo units Nos 165108/10 running through the now disused up main platform with a fast service from Oxford. The two towers in view are the gas works (left) and the rather ornate water tower (right), of which the latter has recently been converted to flats. The sidings on the right were taken out of use in 1978.
GW Trust/Author

Hayes & Harlington

Ex-Great Western 2-6-2T No 6150 arrives at Hayes & Harlington on 17 May 1959 with a Thames Valley service to Reading. The station footbridge was removed in the early 1970s. The East signalbox was closed on 10 June 1968. Looking from the same spot on 20 November 1993 we see a Class 165 Turbo No 165106 passing through with a semi-fast to Reading. The large structure in the background is the ex-GLC rubbish incinerator which was built in the early 1980s on the site of the Great Western creosote (sleeper) works.
M. Hale/Author

Iver

Ex-Great Western diesel parcels car No W34 pauses at Iver (Bucks) in July 1949. The station which contained four platforms was opened by the Great Western on 1 December 1924. Today only the two relief line platforms are in use. On 20 November 1993 Class 165 Turbo No 165123 arrives with a Thames Line service to Reading. The attractive waiting rooms were constructed during the 1980s.
A. A. Delicata/Author

Burnham Beeches
The station at Burnham Beeches was opened by the Great Western on 1 July 1899. These three shots show the station in 1921, 1959 and 1993. As can be seen, the station comprises a single island platform entered via a subway. Burnham box seen on the left in the first picture was closed on 17 November 1962. The second view, taken on 15 May 1959, shows '6100' class 2-6-2T No 6117 arriving with a Thames Valley stopping service to London. In recent years the station has been partially refurbished. On 20 November 1993 Class 165 Turbo No 165137 calls with a service to Reading.
GW Trust/M. Hale/Author

Maidenhead
Maidenhead is the junction station for the old Wycombe Railway branch to Bourne End. In this view taken in July 1963 'Castle' class No 7002 *Devizes Castle* speeds through with a service from Hereford to Paddington. An up parcels train hauled by 2-6-0 No 6309 stands at the up relief platform. The Wycombe bay is on the right.

Apart from the modern lighting the station shows little change, although the down main platform is now unused and as can be seen has been partially removed. Standing at the up relief platform is Turbo No 166219 on a Thames Line semi-fast service from Bedwyn to Paddington.
P. J. Lynch/Author

Furze Platt Halt

Furze Platt Halt was opened by the Great Western on 5 July 1937 to serve the growing community north of Maidenhead. Unusually the halt was provided with a wooden waiting room instead of the standard pagoda. On 1 July 1962 '4800' class 0-4-2T No 1445 pauses with the 12.14pm service from Maidenhead to Marlow. In recent years the branch has been modernised and on 11 December 1993 Class 165 No 165002 stops at the new concrete platform with the 12.10pm service from Marlow to Maidenhead.
L. Sandler/Author

Cookham

Cookham station was opened by the Wycombe Railway on 1 August 1854. It is seen here in September 1954 as an ex-Great Western diesel railcar No W13 arrives with a service from Marlow to Maidenhead.

In recent years the station has been reduced to a single platform, the down side being used as a car park. Much of the old station building is now in private use. On 9 October 1993 Turbo No 165003 arrives with a service from Marlow to Maidenhead.
Real Photos/Author

Bourne End

Bourne End was, and still is, the junction station for the branch to Marlow. The station was opened as Marlow Road on 1 August 1854 but was renamed Bourne End on 1 January 1874. In this 1950s picture, ex-Great Western '4800' class 0-4-2T No 1448 prepares to depart with a service to Marlow.

Yes, this is the same station, pictured here on 9 October 1993. The Marlow service on this occasion was in the hands of Turbo unit No 165003.
J. D. Edwards/Author

Bourne End
From Bourne End the line continued through to High Wycombe. In the late 1950s a '6100' class 2-6-2T No 6131 approaches Bourne End with a service from High Wycombe to Maidenhead.

The section between here and High Wycombe was closed on 4 May 1970, and Bourne End North box was closed on 22 August 1971 when the crossing was removed.

Today, as already mentioned, the line from Maidenhead terminates here. The trackbed of the Wycombe section now forms a road into a small industrial estate.
J. D. Edwards/Author

Marlow

The attractive station at Marlow seen here on 17 February 1962 as '4800' class 0-4-2T No 1421 waits to depart with the 12.20pm service to Maidenhead. The station was opened by the Great Marlow Railway on 27 June 1873. Notice the three different designs of gas lamps on the platform. To cover the 'Then and Now' at Marlow requires three photographs, for the station at Marlow has been moved.

The first shot shows the site of the old station; the main reference point is the house in the centre which can be seen in both pictures. The new entrance to the new station can be seen on the right. The single platform station was opened on 10 July 1967, and is screened by an enormous row of conifers. On 11 December 1993 Class 165 No 165002 waits to depart with the 12.10pm service to Maidenhead.
L. Sandler/Author

Twyford
Twyford is the junction station for the Henley-on-Thames branch. This view from the adjacent road overbridge shows the station around the 1920s. The first station at Twyford was opened here on 1 July 1839 and was a much simpler affair than the station pictured here which was constructed during the quadrupling of the lines through the Thames Valley in 1892/3. Since the introduction of HSTs the main line platforms at Twyford are not used. Thames Line services stopping at Twyford now use the relief platforms. Most Henley branch services still depart from the bay at the west end of the up relief platform. On 9 October 1993 Thames Turbo No 166218 speeds through with an Oxford to Paddington service.
Lens of Sutton/Author

Henley-on-Thames

The branch from Twyford to Henley-on-Thames was opened on 1 June 1857. The station is pictured here in the 1950s. Standing at platform 1 is ex-Great Western 0-6-0PT No 9403 with a service to Twyford and Reading. The station at this time had two main platforms and a bay. The overall roof which survived until 1975 can just be seen at the terminus end. The large building on the left is the Imperial Hotel.

During 1985 the station was reduced to a single platform and a new entrance building was constructed. On 9 October 1993 Thames Turbo No 165113 stands at Henley with the 11.06am service to Reading.
GW Trust/Author

Wargrave

The Henley-on-Thames branch was doubled in 1898 and on 1 January 1900 a new station was opened at Wargrave. The station is pictured here, probably around 1910. With the run-down of services over the branch the line was singled in June 1961 and at the same time the down platform at Wargrave was closed.

The down platform together with the main station building was removed during 1985, the latter being replaced by a simple bus-type shelter.
GW Trust/Author

Reading

Reading station viewed from the west in about 1919. The station seen here was constructed between 1898/1900 and replaced the original one-sided station which had been opened on 30 March 1840.

Apart from some refurbishment work to the platforms, the station has changed little in this view taken on 20 November 1993.
Real Photos/Author

Reading
On 5 August 1939 an ex-Great Western '2251' class 0-6-0 No 2252 stands at Reading with a service from Weymouth to Paddington. The 0-6-0 had replaced a failed 'Hall' at Newbury.
    Today Newbury services are in the hands of Turbo units. On 20 November 1993 No 165106 arrives with a Newbury-Paddington service. The large footbridge was built in 1989 and connects all platforms to the car park and the Brunel Arcade entrance complex. *GW Trust/Author*

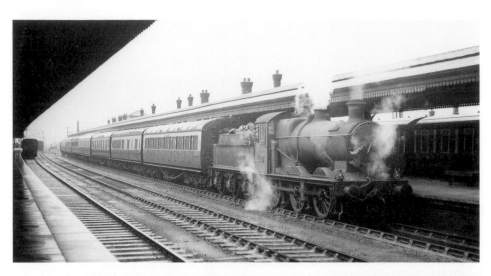

Newbury Race-course
Newbury Race-course station pictured here in the 1920s. The station, which stands adjacent to the race-course, was opened by the Great Western on 26 October 1905. The East Junction Signalbox seen on the right was closed on 14 January 1978. The two views are slightly different as the platforms here were shortened in June 1977 and at the same time the footbridge was moved further west. The East Junction signalbox seen on the right in picture 1 was closed on 14 March 1978. The second picture was taken on 19 January 1994 and shows a pair of '166' Turbo Units on services to and from Bedwyn. Apart from the two main line platforms only one other platform is now in use.
GW Trust/Author

Oxford Road junction
'Hall' class 4-6-0 No 6906 *Chicheley Hall* crosses Oxford Road junction on its approach to Reading West station with a through service from Bradford to Bournemouth in July 1955. The east curve was opened on 21 December 1847 and the west curve on 22 December 1856. Surprisingly a station at Reading West was not opened until 1 July 1906. Oxford Road Junction signalbox, seen here on the left, closed on 25 April 1965.

Looking from the same spot on 11 December 1993 as Class 166 No 166201 accelerates through Reading West with a semi-fast service from Paddington to Bedwyn. In the background is part of the Thames Turbo Reading Triangle depot.
C. L. R. Coles/Author

Tilehurst

'Hall' class No 5901 *Hazel Hall* pulls into Tilehurst on 26 April 1959 with an Oxford-Paddington stopping service. Tilehurst was quite a late addition to Thames Valley stations, not being opened until 1882. The village itself has now grown to become a suburb of Reading. Looking from the same viewpoint on 11 December 1993, a Class 47 No 47241 runs through with the 05.30am Crewe Basford Hall-Southampton freightliner. *M. Hale/Author*

Goring & Streatley

Goring & Streatley station pictured here on 22 May 1963. The photograph shows the relief lines and the main station entrance. The original station here was enlarged during 1893 when the line between Cholsey and Goring was quadrupled. As with all intermediate stations between Reading and Didcot the main line platforms are now closed.

On 11 December 1993 Class 47 No 47204 speeds through with the 04.42am Crewe Basford Hall-Southampton freightliner service. *M. Hale/Author*

Newbury
The 11.30am service from Paddington to Plymouth hauled by 'King' class 4-6-0 No 6029 *King Edward VIII* departs from Newbury in August 1961. Since this picture was taken a certain amount of rationalisation has taken place at Newbury but the station itself has luckily remained almost intact. The two bay platforms at the west end were taken out of use in October 1965 (up-side) and April 1978 (down-side). The West signalbox was closed on 17 April 1978.
    The scene is recreated on a bitterly cold Saturday, 12 February 1994 with both platforms occupied by Thames Turbo units.
B. H. Kimber/Author

Cholsey & Moulsford

An unidentified 'Hall' pulls into Cholsey & Moulsford on 14 May 1951 with a Paddington-Oxford service. On the left a '4800' class 0-4-2T No 1447 waits in the bay with the connecting service for Wallingford. The Wallingford branch was closed to passengers on 15 June 1959 but remained open as a long siding to serve the Allied British Maltsters depot until 28 May 1981. The branch has since been taken over by the Cholsey & Wallingford Preservation Society which hopes to run trains into the bay once more.

Since the introduction of the HSTs the main line platforms at Cholsey (Moulsford has now been dropped) have been closed and fenced off. On 4 December 1993 Class 37 No 37068 *Grainflow* runs through with an empty ballast train.
R. C. Riley/Author

Wallingford

'4800' class 0-4-2T No 1444 together with its autocoach stands outside the small engine shed at Wallingford on 19 April 1952. The engine shed was closed on 11 February 1956; passenger services were withdrawn on 15 June 1959 but the station remained open for goods traffic until 13 September 1965. Since then a housing estate and access road have been built on the station site. The one remaining reference point is the large gabled house seen in the centre of both pictures.
R. J. Doran/Author

Moreton Cutting yard

Moreton Cutting yard was situated just to the east of Didcot. It was was opened on 11 April 1941 and is seen here on 4 July 1953 as 'Grange' class 4-6-0 No 6805 *Broughton Grange* runs past with some down milk empties.

The yard was closed on 10 August 1964. Since then the area has become somewhat overgrown; Class 165 No 165104 passes with a Thames Line stopping service.
R. C. Riley/Author

Didcot engine shed

A view of Didcot engine shed in 1963, with from left to right '6100' class 2-6-2Ts Nos 6136 and 6159 and '4300' class 2-6-0 No 5380. Also in the shot is an '08' diesel and a 'Modified Hall'. The shed which was opened by the Great Western in June 1932 was closed to steam on 14 June 1965 but continued to be used by BR until 1969 as a diesel stabling point. Since 1969 'Didcot Railway Centre', as it is now known, has been the home of the Great Western Society. The shed is seen here on 14 November 1993 as preserved '4800' class 0-4-2T No 1466 and '4500' class 2-6-2T No 5572 are prepared for the days work.
Author's Collection/Author

Didcot

Didcot is one location that has seen considerable change in recent years. Looking west from the Foxhall bridge towards Foxhall junction on 7 June 1960: a pair of coaches are seen being slipped from the 7am service from Weston-super-Mare to Paddington. This was the last multiple slip working in the country. Foxhall Junction box was opened on 13 October 1931; it was closed on 17 May 1965. The scene has changed somewhat with the towers of Didcot power station, opened in September 1970, dominating the skyline. On 4 December 1993 an HST arrives with the 11.54am service from Weston-super-Mare. Foxhall junction can just be seen behind the front power car. Notice also the new signal gantry.
J. Coiley/Author

Challow

Faringdon Road station was opened by the Great Western on 20 July 1840, it was renamed Challow on 1 June 1864. The station was rebuilt in 1932, when the two-track layout was widened to four and the platforms were lengthened. The station is pictured here in the early 1960s as ex-works 'Grange' class 4-6-0 No 6826 *Nannerth Grange* arrives with a Swindon-Didcot stopping service. The station was closed on 7 December 1964 and the platform loops were removed. During this last year the loops have been reinstated in preparation for the Avonmouth-Didcot coal trains. The new formation is seen here on 11 January 1994 as a Bristol-Paddington HST service speeds past. *GW Trust/Peter Heath*

Shrivenham
A 'Modified Hall' class 4-6-0 No 7902 *Eaton Mascot Hall* speeds through Shrivenham on 5 August 1950 with the 4.35pm service from Kingswear to Paddington (via Bristol) service. The station was closed to passengers on 7 December 1964. On 11 January 1994 an HST on a service from Bristol to Paddington speeds past the remains of the platforms. The building in the background has been constructed in recent years on the site of the old goods shed.
P. Wells/Peter Heath

Culham

Back to the Oxford line as an up stopping service from Oxford to Reading pulls into Culham station in August 1958 behind 'Hall' class 4-6-0 No 5983 *Henley Hall*. The station was opened on 12 June 1844 as Abingdon Road but was renamed Culham on 2 June 1856. Notice the ex-broad gauge goods shed on the left. The signalbox was closed on 15 February 1961, and the goods shed and down side buildings were removed in 1972. The Brunel designed up-side building, seen on both pictures, is listed. During September 1993 a new up platform was constructed at Culham and is seen here on 4 December 1993 as Class 166 No 166217 runs through with the 12 noon service from Oxford to Paddington.

J. D. Edwards/Author

Radley

Radley station was opened on 8 September 1873. The station is pictured here in the 1940s as 'Saint' class 4-6-0 No 2912 *St Ambrose* arrives with an up stopping service. The Abingdon branch bay is on the left. The small signalbox on the up platform was closed on 23 May 1965 and the station buildings were demolished during the same year. The Abingdon branch was closed to passenger traffic on 9 September 1963 but survived for goods traffic until 30 June 1984. Today Radley is an unstaffed halt, the main entrance area on the up-side has now been sold, and the only entrance to the up platform is via the footbridge (ideal if you are disabled!). On 8 January 1994 an HST speeds through Radley with the 'Cotswold & Malvern Express' service to London.
R. G. H. Simpson/Author

Littlemore

Littlemore station looking east on 13 August 1959. The station was opened on 24 October 1864 and was the first station on the Oxford-Princes Risborough branch after leaving Oxford. The large building on the right was the county lunatic asylum but is now the Littlemore Psychiatric Hospital. For many years this establishment had its own private coal siding. The station was closed to passengers on 7 January 1963 and to goods on 21 June 1971. The line is still open as far as the Morris Cowley International Freight Terminal. On 10 December 1993 Class 37 No 37261 runs down the branch with the '6M90' 10.15am service from Morris Cowley to Bescot Yard. *GW Trust/Author*

Oxford

Looking north from the Becket Street footbridge in 1958, a '7200' class 2-8-2T No 7247 runs through Oxford on an up freight. Standing in the up goods loop is ex-LMS Class 8F No 48476. On the left are the West Midland sidings and on the right Becket Street yard. The station which was opened on 1 October 1852 originally had an overall roof but this was removed when the station was rebuilt in 1891. The station survived almost intact until 1970 when it was again rebuilt. This new 'temporary' station was demolished in 1989 and replaced by the new brick structure that we can see today. The scene has changed somewhat as Class 47 No 47839 departs on 7 January 1994 with a Liverpool-Paddington service. Becket Street yard closed on 28 October 1977. The remains of the old West Midland sidings, although still *in situ*, have not been used for a number of years.
J. D. Edwards/Author

Bletchington
An unidentified 'Hall' on a through service from Birkenhead to Poole approaches Bletchington on 24 August 1963. The station was opened as Woodstock Road in May 1851; it was renamed Kirtlington in July 1855 and Bletchington on 11 August 1890. Bletchington was closed on 2 November 1964 and today only the old stationmaster's house remains (right) as Turbo No 165108 speeds through with a morning service from Banbury. *J. Spencer-Gilks/Author*

Fritwell & Somerton

The attractive station at Fritwell & Somerton was situated on the Oxford-Banbury line just to the south of Aynho. The station, pictured here in 1919, was opened in 1855 as Somerton, but was renamed Fritwell & Somerton in October 1907. The small signalbox, at the end of the down platform, was closed on 18 September 1966. The station was closed to passengers on 2 November 1964, and the platforms have since been removed; but part of the station fencing can still be seen as Thames Turbo No 166219 speeds through on 18 April 1994 en-route to Oxford. *Real Photos/Author*

Aynho

'Grange' class 4-6-0 No 6871 *Bourton Grange* speeds through Aynho for Deddington on 8 August 1964 with the 9.5am service from Wolverhampton LL to Portsmouth Harbour. Aynho was opened on 2 September 1850 with the opening of the line from Oxford to Banbury. With the opening of Aynho Park Platform, on the high level line in 1910, the low level station at Aynho had the suffix 'for Deddington' added to the running-in boards. As with many other stations on the Oxford-Banbury line Aynho was closed on 2 November 1964. The signalbox was closed on 16 September 1968. The only remaining part of the station, the down-side building, is listed and has recently been up for sale. On 18 April 1994 Class 47 No 47826 accelarates away from a PW slack with the 11.6am service from Birmingham New Street to Paddington. *S. Creer/Author*

Gerrards Cross

The 12.38pm service from Princes Risborough to Paddington hauled by '6100' class 2-6-2T No 6157 stands at Gerrards Cross on 7 May 1960. Standing at the down platform is a Marylebone-High Wycombe service. The cutting at this point is about 60ft deep which required the up-side station entrance to be built on two levels.

During the 1970s the two fast lines were removed, and with the Chiltern Line modernisation during 1989 the up platform was extended outwards and the old up platform line was slewed outwards to the approximate position of the old down main. The new layout at Gerrards Cross is shown to good effect in this picture of Turbo Class 165 No 165022 as it waits with a High Wycombe-Marylebone service on 30 October 1993.
D. Trevor Rowe/Author

Beaconsfield

It really is quite remarkable just how little some locations have changed. One such place is Beaconsfield pictured here in June 1961 as an unidentified 'Castle' speeds through with a down Wolverhampton service.

Some 32 years later the motive power has changed and the through fast roads have been removed but apart from some refurbishment work the station has changed little.

W. Turner/Author

High Wycombe

A good vantage point for photographers is the footbridge across the brick cutting just to the north of High Wycombe station. Here in 1957 ex-streamlined 'King' No 6014 *King Henry VII* accelerates away through High Wycombe with a service to Birkenhead. The undergrowth on the right has meant a higher viewpoint has to be used today as Turbo unit No 165038 departs with the 11.40am service to Banbury on 19 June 1993. The graffiti on the wall are now a reminder of Mrs Thatcher's poll tax fiasco.
J. D. Edwards/Author

High Wycombe

Looking northwards from the same footbridge on 31 July 1956 we see 'King' class No 6022 *King Edward III* winding its way into High Wycombe with the 3.00pm service from Birmingham Snow Hill to Paddington.

The trackwork has now been altered at this point to allow two-way working at High Wycombe. On 19 June 1993 Turbo unit No 165036 approaches the station on the 11.30am Banbury-Marylebone service.
R. M. Newland/Author

Princes Risborough

Looking from the roadbridge at the south end of Princes Risborough in 1950 ex-Great Western 'Star' class 4-6-0 No 4060 *Princess Eugenie* starts the climb up to Saunderton Summit with an up Birmingham service. Notice the upper quadrant signal reminding us that this stretch of the route was an LNER/GW joint line.

On 19 June 1993 Turbo unit No 165035 leaves Princes Risborough with the 12.30pm service from Banbury to Marylebone. The up relief line has long been removed whilst the down relief is now used as a long siding for engineering trains. *Ian Allan Library/ Author*

Princes Risborough
An ex-LNER 'L1' 2-6-4T No 67800 and an ex-Great Western 0-6-0PT No 7763 stand in the bay platform at Princes Risborough with an Aylesbury branch service on 13 September 1955. The 'L1' interestingly carries a 34A (King's Cross) shedplate.

Today the bay platform is still open but is generally used for stabling purposes with most trains running from Aylesbury through to Marylebone. However, on Saturdays a local shuttle service still operates between Princes Risborough and Aylesbury. Here on 19 June 1993 two-car Turbo set No 165022 stands in the bay with the 5.20pm (SO) service to Aylesbury.
S. Creer/Author

Aylesbury

Aylesbury was the terminus of the old Wycombe Railway route from Maidenhead via Princes Risborough. The line which was opened on 1 October 1863 was subsequently taken over by the Great Western. In this 1950s shot 0-4-2T No 1473 has just arrived at the down bay platform with the autotrain from Princes Risborough. The 'B1' No 61001 *Eland* is standing in the shed yard. The loco shed at Aylesbury was jointly operated by the Great Central and the Great Western, being a sub shed of both Neasden and Slough. It was closed on 16 June 1962.

The Aylesbury-Princes Risborough service still runs today and on 30 October 1993 was being operated by Turbo No 165018. I have increased the angle to show more of the recently renovated station.
D. Lawrence/Author

Chinnor

One branch that seems to have a bright future is the remains of the Watlington branch between Princes Risborough and Chinnor. The branch was closed to passenger traffic on 1 June 1957 but remained open for coal traffic as far as Chinnor cement works until 1990. The line was then taken over by the Princes Risborough & Chinnor Railway Society which hopes to reopen the line in the not too distant future. The present terminus of the line is at Chinnor, pictured here around the turn of the century and before the construction of the cement works in 1908. The station was opened on 15 August 1872 and was closed on 1 July 1957. The second picture taken on 16 April 1994 shows the new platform almost complete.
Author's collection/Author

Chinnor Station.

Thame

Thame was the main intermediate station on the Oxford-Princes Risborough branch. It was opened by the Wycombe Railway on 2 August 1862. A feature of the station which survived until closure was the Brunel-designed overall roof. It is seen to good effect in this picture of a 'Hall' class 4-6-0 No 6990 *Witherslack Hall* departing with the 11.30am Oxford-Paddington via Maidenhead stopping service. Although the line was closed to passengers in 1963 the section between Thame oil terminal and Princes Risborough remained open until September 1991. The yard on the right is now an industrial site. As the increasing undergrowth has made the same angle difficult, I have taken the picture from the adjacent road overbridge to show the way nature is taking over.
J. E. Norris/Author

Blackthorn Station, Bicester

Blackthorn

Blackthorn was situated just south of Bicester, and is seen here probably soon after opening in 1910. Those who know the area may wonder why the Great Western built such a large station to serve a village that in 1910 had a population of about 100. It was the company's idea of course to do a 'Metropolitan', and expand the commuting area out into rural Oxfordshire. Fortunately or unfortunately (whichever way you look at it) it did not happen. Blackthorn never saw much passenger traffic and was closed on 8 June 1953.

Today the only trace of the station is the road entrance which is on the right behind the trees. The Great Western gate posts are still *in situ* but today the road leads to a builder's yard.
Author's Collection/Author

Bicester North

The down platform at Bicester North station around 1920. The station was opened together with the new 'cut-off route' to Birmingham on 1 July 1910; notice that the up platform is constructed of wood. The large goods shed was closed in 1964 but was not removed for a number of years. The signalbox was closed on 27 October 1968 and during the same month the line between Princes Risborough and Aynho junction was singled. There was even talk of closure north of Princes Risborough. Luckily this never happened and with the subsequent modernisation of the 'Chiltern Line' Bicester is busy once again. It is now the only passing point on the Aynho-Risborough section of the route.

The refurbished station is seen here on 10 October 1993.
Authors Collection/Author

Ardley

'King' class 4-6-0 No 6011 *King James I* passes through Ardley station with the 1.10pm service from Paddington to Wolverhampton on 26 May 1962. The station was opened with the line on 1 July 1910. Passenger traffic was never very busy and for many years the station was only served by the Banbury-Princes Risborough auto-service. The line was singled between Bicester and Aynho junction during November 1968. Today only the remains of the down platform remain as Chiltern Turbo No 165032 speeds past with the 10.40am Marylebone-Banbury service.
D. Trevor Rowe/Author

Aynho Park Platform

Aynho Park Platform was opened on 1 July 1910 and was situated at the north end of the 'cut-off route' or 'New Road' between Ardley and Aynho junction. The platform stood only a short distance from the lower level station, Aynho for Deddington, whose stationmaster was responsible for both stations. Aynho Park was closed on 7 January 1963.

Today the spot is marked by the milepost and the abutments of the roadbridge which can be seen in both pictures.
Ian Allan Library/Author

King's Sutton

The attractive station at King's Sutton seen here on 7 February 1962. The station building with its ornate chimneys was opened on 2 August 1872, and really should have been listed; unfortunately this was not the case and the building together with the footbridge was demolished in the 1970s. Only the small building on the down side remains as Turbo No 165034 arrives with a Marylebone service on 30 October 1993.
G. J. Biddle/Author

King's Sutton

Looking south from the small overbridge at King's Sutton, 'Castle' class No 5076 *Gladiator* approaches the station with a service to Wolverhampton. Running in from the right is the Banbury-Cheltenham direct line. This ceased to be a through route from 3 December 1963 when the section between Chipping Norton and Hook Norton was closed due to a landslip. The section seen above remained open for freight as far as Adderbury until 4 December 1967.

By slightly altering the angle it is still possible to see the abutments of the small viaduct (right) that carried the line over the River Cherwell. The Turbo unit is Class 165 No 165037 on a Chiltern Line stopping service.
GW Trust/Peter Heath

Chipping Norton

An unidentified '5100' class 2-6-2T waits at Chipping Norton with an afternoon service to Kingham in 1961. The through line from Banbury to Cheltenham was effectively operated as a branch between Kingham and Chipping Norton with the withdrawal of through passenger services between Banbury and Kingham on 4 June 1951. Chipping Norton was closed to passengers on 3 December 1962 and to freight on 7 September 1964 and today the station site is in use as a builder's merchants; part of the down platform can still be seen on the right. The old goods yard now forms the 'Station Industrial Estate'.

W. J. K. Davies/Author

Banbury

This view of Banbury was taken from the adjacent road overbridge on 6 August 1960 and shows, on the left, a new WR DMU arriving at the up platform with the 7.5pm service to Reading. In the centre 'Hall' class 4-6-0 No 6934 *Beachamwell Hall* departs with the 3.40pm service from Portsmouth Harbour to Wolverhampton, whilst fellow class member No 6931 *Aldborough Hall* waits in the bay. The original station at Banbury was opened in 1850 but the station seen here was constructed in 1957/8 under the Western Region's modernisation plan.

On 1 November 1993 Class 47 No 47849 departs with the 9.5am service from Poole to York. The through line on the right is now used by Chiltern Line services and apart from the south end bay all other bay platforms are unused.

M. Mensing/Peter Heath

Banbury

A busy summer's evening at Banbury in 1961. On the right a through service from the south coast to the Midlands is double-headed by a pair of 'Hall' class 4-6-0s Nos 5947 *St Benet's Hall* and 6906 *Chicheley Hall*. Approaching the station is 'King' No 6008 *King James II* with the 4.20pm service from Wolverhampton.

On 1 November 1993 Turbo unit No 165032 departs with the 12.9pm service to Birmingham Snow Hill. The various north end bay platforms are now unused but at the time of writing Banbury North signalbox is still in operation.

W. Turner/Peter Heath

Section 2
Somerset and Avon

Somerset, Dorset, Wilts and Avon

This area was once covered by a number of branch lines but the widespread closures of the 1960s mean almost none is left. In Somerset, sections of the Frome-Radstock and the Witham-Yatton lines are still used for stone traffic. There are also two preserved lines, the West Somerset Railway from Norton Fitzwarren (or for regular services Bishops Lydeard) to Minehead and the East Somerset Railway at Cranmore which is part of the Witham-Yatton line.

The Great Western foothold in Dorset was centred around the Yeovil-Weymouth line. Although the line was singled during the summer of 1968, and has in recent years seen little investment, it still continues to provide an important cross-country route to the south coast. There were only two other ex-Great Western branches in the county. The Weymouth-Abbotsbury branch closed as long ago as 1 December 1952 but the delightful Maiden Newton-Bridport branch survived until 5 May 1975.

Wiltshire was at one time quite well served by the Great Western with branches to Calne, Highworth, Malmesbury and Devizes and also the Midland & South Western Junction route from Cheltenham to Andover, all (alas) now gone. However, a short section of the M&SWJR between Blunsdon and Cricklade is now operated by the Swindon & Cricklade Railway Society. Swindon was at one time the most important engineering centre on the Great Western but since the end of steam traction in 1965, and the closure of the Works in 1986, it has become just another stopping-point for InterCity services

The county of Avon was formed in 1974 and incorporates parts of north Somerset,

Wiltshire and south Gloucestershire. Within the county is the city of Bristol, still one of the most important centres on the ex-Great Western lines. Temple Meads is the second largest station on the system and has recently undergone an extensive (and expensive) refurbishment programme particulary concentrating on Francis Fox's superb overall roof. A new Parkway station, built on the site of Stoke Gifford yard on the South Wales main line to the north of the city, was opened on 1 May 1972. During 1993 the branch line to Avonmouth Docks has been upgraded to deal with imported coal traffic for Didcot power station. This has also resulted in the provision of new relief lines between Swindon and Didcot. The large locomotive depot at Bristol Bath Road deals with a variety of locomotives including a large number of InterCity sector Class 47s. At St Philip's Marsh a purpose-built depot on the site of the old steam shed deals with HST servicing and repairs. Many local lines are still open, although the Portishead branch was closed to passengers on 7 September 1964. For the steam fan the Avon Valley Railway operates over a short section of the ex-Midland Railway's Mangotsfield-Bath line.

In Wiltshire the Bathampton, Westbury and Salisbury line still forms part of an important through route connecting Southampton to Bristol and South Wales. Of the other lines in the county the Bristol-Radstock line was closed to passengers on 2 November 1959; although it remained open for goods until November 1965. The Limpley Stoke-Camerton branch closed on 15 February 1951, becoming famous in the early 1950s when it was used for the 'Titfield

Thunderbolt' film. The line from Trowbridge to Devizes and Patney was closed to passengers on 18 April 1966 and the short branch from Chippenham to Calne on 20 September 1965. The line from Thingley junction to Trowbridge was closed on 18 April 1966 but, luckily, was retained for diversionary use and wagon storage. On 13 May 1985 a Swindon-Melksham service was reinstated, initially as an experiment, but has obviously been successful as it is still in operation and has been extended through to Westbury.

The area is well served by main line services. To the north the South Wales main line passes through Wiltshire and Avon. The Bristol line diverges away at Wootton Bassett junction and passes through Wilts, Avon and Somerset. The West of England main line runs via Westbury passing through

Previous page: Two GWR publicity posters from the GW Trust's collection.

Wiltshire and Somerset to join the Bristol line at Cogload junction. The Paddington-Cheltenham HST services run via Swindon and Kemble. Intermediate passenger services in the four counties are operated by Regional Railways using Class 143, 150, 153 and 168 units, with main line InterCity services in the hands of Class 47s and HSTs.

Freight services consist mostly of oil, coal and aggre-gate traffic. Trainloads of aggr-egate from the Mendip quarries are sorted and despatched from the Westbury area. These are hauled by Classes 37, 56, 60 and the privately-owned Class 59s.

Stratton

Stratton station was the first station out of Swindon on the single line branch to Highworth, and is pictured here in 1959. The station looks in remarkably good condition considering that it was closed to passengers on 2 March 1953. How long would it last in this condition today? The branch remained open for goods traffic as far as Stratton until 4 October 1965. The old station site is now in use as a haulage depot, the only reference point being the house in the centre left.

J. D. Edwards /Peter Heath

Highworth

The branch terminated at Highworth where in June 1952 '4800' class 0-4-2T No 1403 waits to depart with a service to Swindon. Highworth was also closed to passenger traffic on 2 March 1953 but remained open for goods until 6 August 1962. Since then the whole site has been swallowed up by a large housing estate. Even the stationmaster's house, seen behind the second coach, has been demolished. The road in the foreground was built on the trackbed of the branch.
J. B. Snell/Peter Heath

Swindon

Swindon station was opened by the Great Western on 17 December 1840. It became a junction with the opening of the line to Kemble in May 1841. The station is pictured here in 1909. On the right is the bay platform for the Trowbridge line and Swindon Town services.

The down-side platform was closed and removed in 1976. Its site now forms part of a slip road into the station car park. The large building on the right is the headquarters of an insurance company. The remaining island platform is now used by both up and down services, with a west bay retained for Gloucester line trains. Notice also that only part of the original building on this platform has been retained. The present layout can be seen to good effect in this picture taken on 18 August 1993 of Class 60 No 60064 *Back Tor* with the down Colnbrook-Milford Haven oil empties.
C. Maggs/Author

Swindon Works

In 1985, the 150th anniversary year of the Great Western, it was announced that the locomotive works that had been established at Swindon in 1843 would close. During 1987 the site was sold to Tarmac Properties and in the last few years many of the buildings including the mighty 'A Shop' have been demolished. Apart from the original works building which is listed, another historic item to remain is the 65ft turntable which stood adjacent to the Rodbourne Road entrance. It is seen alongside ex-works 2-8-0 No 4257 on 7 February 1960.

On 22 October 1993 the turntable stands alone.
Dr G. Smith/Peter Heath

Swindon Town

The other station at Swindon was Swindon Town. This was also the headquarters of the Midland & South Western Junction Railway whose offices can be seen on the right. On 9 July 1951 'Manor' No 7824 *Iford Manor* arrives with a service from Cheltenham to Southampton; also in shot is 0-6-0PT No 9600 on a goods service to Swindon junction.

Town station was closed to passengers on 11 September 1961 but the line remained open for goods traffic until 1 November 1966. The station area is now a small industrial estate but part of the old M&SWJ offices can still be seen on the right.
R. C. Riley/Author

Chiseldon

Chiseldon was situated on the old M&SWJ line south of Swindon. The rather attractive station is pictured here on 31 August 1959. The station together with the line was closed on 11 September 1961. Since closure the station site has been converted into a children's play area. Part of the abutment of the bridge is still *in situ* and can just be seen on the right.
GW Trust/Author

Marlborough Low Level

A Swindon-Andover service hauled by '4300' class 2-6-0 No 5367 stands at Marlborough Low Level (M&SWJR) in August 1950. The Great Western station at Marlborough High Level was closed on 6 March 1933 and from that date services from Savernake Low Level used the Low Level station seen here. Marlborough Low Level closed to passengers on 11 September 1961 but remained open for goods until 7 September 1964. After closure the station area was taken over by the Wiltshire County Council who now use the site as a highways depot. The hill in the background is the reference point on this picture taken on 21 October 1993.
Real Photos/Peter Heath

Ludgershall

Beyond Savernake the M&SWJ ran via Ludgershall to connect with the LSWR main line at Andover junction. At Ludgershall a small branch served the military camp at Tidworth. Ludgershall was closed to passengers on 11 September 1961 but remained open for freight traffic until 24 March 1969. The closed station can be seen as BR Standard Class 4 No 75003 runs through with a northbound freight on 19 September 1962. The line remains open from Andover junction to serve the military establishments at Ludgershall and Tidworth. The remains of the station are seen here on 21 October 1993. Currently a number of preserved Class 33 locomotives are stored on the branch. *D. Cross/Peter Heath*

Chippenham

'King' class 4-6-0 No 6019 *King Henry V* arrives at Chippenham on 24 March 1951 with the 9.5am service from Paddington to Bristol. The down main platform at Chippenham is now unused with all trains using the island platform. In October 1993 an HST prepares to leave with a Bristol-Paddington service. The gas works has now gone but the large building of Westinghouse Brakes Ltd still dominates the scene. *G. J. Jefferson/Author*

Bathampton

'Grange' class No 6850 *Cleeve Grange* pauses at Bathampton station with a Bristol-Swindon service in the early 1960s. The engine is on an ex-works running in turn. Bathampton was the junction for the line to Trowbridge and Westbury.

Looking east the junction can be seen diverging away to the right as ex-Great Western 0-6-0PT No 8730 runs through the station with a down goods service on 14 August 1954.

Bathampton station was closed on 3 August 1966 and is now gone but the junction is still busy. Here on a sunny October morning Class 158 No 158823 leaves the Westbury line with a Portsmouth-Cardiff service. *Hugh Ballantyne/M. J. Fox/Author*

Freshford

The picturesque station at Freshford is situated south of Bathampton on the Trowbridge-Westbury line. On 3 May 1958 'Castle' class No 4084 *Aberystwyth Castle* pulls away with a Westbury to Bristol stopping service.

Today the cutting is overgrown so the 'now' shot was taken from the garden of the old station house. The station itself is now an unstaffed halt and trains stop by request. The unidentified Sprinter is running through on a service to Weymouth on 10 October 1993. *R. E. Toop/Author*

Avoncliff Halt

The next station along the line is at Avoncliff Halt, pictured here in the 1950s with 2-8-2T No 7202 passing through with an up goods. The double span bridge carries the Kennet & Avon Canal over the railway at this point.

The second picture was taken on 10 October 1993, and shows how little the scene has changed. The short platforms are now ideal for the two-coach units that work the passenger services over this line. Notice also the ex-Great Western seat on the up platform.

R. E. Toop/Author

Westbury

Westbury station on 15 June 1963 as 'Castle' class 4-6-0 No 5043 *Earl of Mount Edgcombe* leaves with the 4.33pm service from Salisbury to Bristol, whilst 'Hall' No 6930 *Aldersley Hall* waits with the 5.25pm service to Swindon. Apart from being situated on the ex-Great Western West of England main line, Westbury is a major interchange point and junction for cross-country services from Cardiff and Bristol to Portsmouth and Weymouth. Westbury has now become a busy staging point for aggregate traffic from the nearby stone quarries.

During the mid-1980s a new power box was opened at Westbury and all mechanical boxes in the area were closed. The station has changed little as Class 37 No 37191 departs with a summer Saturday service from Weymouth to Cardiff on 14 August 1993. *G. T. Robinson/Author*

Yeovil Pen Mill

Yeovil Pen Mill stands on what is still an important cross-country route which runs from Castle Cary to Dorchester and Weymouth. On 18 April 1952 ex-Great Western 0-6-0 No 2213 waits at the platform with a service to Weymouth. In the yard are a pair of pannier tanks and a '4800' class 0-4-2T with an autocoach. Apart from the removal of a few sidings it's surprising how little change has taken place at Pen Mill. Semaphore signalling is still in evidence as is the North signalbox.
GW Trust/Author

Yeovil Pen Mill

Looking south from the roadbridge an unidentified 'Castle' class leaves Pen Mill with a service to Weymouth. In the centre is the small ex-Great Western engine shed and on the right is the line to Yeovil Town.

On a murky September day the scene has changed considerably; the site of the engine shed which closed on 5 January 1959 is now completely overgrown. The short branch to Yeovil Town closed on 6 May 1968. However, close inspection shows the cattle dock (left) still remains, if somewhat overgrown.

D. Lawrence/Michael Baker

Yeovil Town
The Great Western and London & South Western joint station at Yeovil Town is pictured here on 25 August 1957. Great Western services ran in from Langport and Pen Mill. On the right is the ex-LSWR loco shed, which gained a small allocation of ex-Great Western locomotives after the closure of Pen Mill. Yeovil Town station was closed on 1 March 1967.

Today the site of the station is covered by a car and coach park although proposals are in hand to build a supermarket here. The old roadbridge over the line can just be seen right centre.
C. Boocock/Author

Maiden Newton

Maiden Newton was the junction station for the Bridport branch. In this picture taken on 22 March 1958 'Hall' class 4-6-0 No 5978 *Bodinnick Hall* arrives with a Weymouth-Yeovil service, whilst waiting in the bay with a Bridport service is '4500' class 2-6-2T No 4507.

The Bridport branch closed on 5 May 1975 and today the bay is empty as a Class 150 unit leaves for Weymouth on a murky September day. Notice also the replacement Southern-style concrete footbridge.
C. Boocock/Michael Baker

Weymouth Quay

This nostalgic picture shows an ex-Great Western 0-6-0PT No 7780 heading towards the quay at Weymouth with a short freight on 19 June 1959. Apart from the old fishing boats, just look at the cars! The same scene in September 1993: the quay line is now officially closed but still sees occasional use by enthusiasts' specials.
K. L. Cook/Michael Baker

Bath Spa

'Modified Hall' class 4-6-0 No 6981 *Marbury Hall* arrives at Bath Spa with the 7pm service from Bristol to Westbury on 18 July 1964. The first station at Bath was constructed in August 1840 for the opening of the line from Bristol. The station was rebuilt in 1897 to give a layout very much as we see it today. The elevated signalbox on the down platform was opened in September 1897. It was closed on 21 January 1968 but was not removed until the early 1970s when the station was partially refurbished. Apart from that there is no obvious change as Class 158 No 158871 arrives on 19 August 1993 with a service from Paignton.
C. R. Scunell/Author

Bath Spa
The 2.33pm service from
Portsmouth to Bristol Temple
Meads rolls into Bath Spa on
30 May 1956 hauled by 'County'
class 4-6-0 No 1014 *County of
Glamorgan.*

The same services today run
through to Cardiff and are in the
hands of Class 158 units. Here on
19 September 1993 No 158870
arrives at Bath.
N. Lockett/Author

Bath Spa
A railway enthusiasts'
excursion to Bristol
pulled by 'Hall' class
4-6-0 No 6963 *Throwley
Hall* leaves Bath in
March 1965. The Spa
station can just be seen
on the right.

Owing to the
proliferation of trees the
'today' shot is from a
slightly lower angle and
shows Class 37
No 37705 running
through with some oil
empties on
19 September 1993.
R. E. Toop/Author

Stoke Gifford Yard
Ex-Great Western '7200' class 2-8-2T No 7252 restarts an up permanent way train from Stoke Gifford yard on 17 October 1964. The yard was opened in May 1903 and was enlarged during 1918 to give 14 up and 10 down sidings. The yard was closed on 4 October 1971, the site being used for the construction of Bristol Parkway. The new station was opened on 1 May 1972 and can just be seen in the background as an HST departs with a Paddington service. *E. Thomas/Steven Park*

Pilning

Ex-Great Western '4100' class 2-6-2T No 4151 passes through Pilning on 23 May 1958 with an up freight. Rationalisation has seen the platform buildings removed and today Pilning is an unstaffed halt served by Bristol-Cardiff local services. The station is seen here on 28 November 1993 as an HST speeds through *en route* to Paddington.
M. Hale/Steven Park

Severn Tunnel

The 12.50pm service from Cardiff to Brighton pulled by 'Hall' class 4-6-0 No 4918 *Dartington Hall* emerges from the Severn Tunnel and starts its climb up to Pilning on 10 February 1962.

Apart from the removal of semaphore signalling there is remarkably little change as Regional Railways Class 158 No 158864 approaches Pilning on 28 November 1993 with a through service from Swansea to Portsmouth Harbour.
Hugh Ballantyne/Steven Park

Severn Beach

Severn Beach station stands on what was once a through line from Stapleton Road to Pilning, via Avonmouth. The northern section was closed on 23 November 1964 but surprisingly the section to Severn Beach was retained. It is seen here in the early 1960s when the line to Pilning was still open, crossing the road at this point via the level crossing. Severn Beach is now the terminus of the branch and is pictured here on 28 November 1993 as Class 143 No 143612 waits with the return service to Bristol. *C. Maggs/Steven Park*

Bristol Temple Meads

Bristol Temple Meads

The original terminus at Bristol Temple Meads was opened on 31 August 1840 with the opening of the line to Bath. The large station that we see today was opened on 1 January 1878 and served as a joint station for Great Western, Midland and Bristol & Exeter services. The station was again rebuilt in 1935 with the addition of several new platforms. The first picture is dated December 1935 and shows the new layout at Temple Meads, together with the colour-light signalling that had recently been installed. The second view is taken from approximately the same location on 2 September 1952 and shows 'Britannia' Pacific No 70022 *Tornado* leaving with a service to Plymouth.

   Apart from some track rationalisation the station looks pretty much the same, as two ex-BR Class 20s Nos 20904/1 run through on 16 August 1993 with a weedkilling train. *Ian Allan Library/G Heiron/Author*

Bristol Temple Meads

On 12 July 1957 'Castle' No 5085 *Evesham Abbey* pulls into Bristol Temple Meads with empty stock for the up 'Bristolian', the 4.30pm service to Paddington. Waiting in the siding to take the 1.12pm service from Plymouth northwards is fellow class member No 7037 *Swindon*.

Taken from the same spot on 16 August 1993 Class 158 No 158853 leaves with a service to Milford Haven. Francis Fox's fine 125ft-span overall roof has recently been restored. *J. D. Edwards/Author*

Bristol Bath Road

The large ex-Great Western locomotive depot at Bristol Bath Road, pictured here on 9 July 1960. This shed which stood on the site of the old Bristol & Exeter depot was opened by the GWR in December 1934. It was closed to steam on 12 September 1960 to allow for conversion into a diesel depot.

The new diesel depot was opened on 18 June 1962 and is seen here in September 1993. The depot now maintains a variety of locomotives but notably Class 47s for the parcels sector. At the time of writing it is rumoured that the depot may soon close. *Hugh Ballantyne/Author*

Yatton

As the station running-in board proclaims Yatton was the junction station for the branches to Clevedon and Witham. On 7 September 1963 'Castle' No 7036 *Taunton Castle* arrives with the 9.45am Saturdays-only service from Paddington to Weston-super-Mare. Taking water in the bay is ex-LMS 2-6-2T No 41245 on the 1.45pm service to Witham. This was the last day of steam services between Paddington and Weston-super-Mare and also the last day of services between Yatton and Witham.

The Witham branch was officially closed on 9 September 1963; the Clevedon branch lasted until 3 October 1966. In August 1993 only the up-side canopy survives as single car Class 153 No 153362 arrives with a service from Bristol to Weston-super-Mare.
Hugh Ballantyne/Alan Cornish

Cheddar

Cheddar station stood on the Yatton-Witham branch. On 17 August 1963 an ex-LMS 2-6-2T No 41245 waits at Cheddar with the 3.28pm service from Witham to Yatton. These locomotives saw extensive use on the branch in the late 1950s and early 1960s. The station was constructed of stone and as can be seen was particulary attractive. The line was closed to passenger traffic on 9 September 1963. Some 30 years later the station building remains but the site is being used as a stone yard.
D. H. Ballantyne/Alan Cornish

Wells (Tucker Street)

On a lovely summer's day in the 1950s ex-Great Western 0-6-0PT No 3773 arrives at Wells (Tucker Street) with a service from Yatton to Witham. Tucker Street was closed on 9 September 1963 although the section from Dulcote Quarry to Cheddar remained open for stone traffic until March 1969.

The trackbed can still be seen clearly in this view taken in August 1993. The station yard is now a housing estate but the stone road overbridge, behind the footbridge in the first view, remains.
R. E. Toop/Alan Cornish

Worle junction

The Weston-super-Mare branch leaves the main line to the east at Worle junction. The junction is seen here on 26 March 1956 as 'Castle' No 5089 *Westminster Abbey* joins the main line with the 7am service from Paignton to Liverpool. The remains of Worle Junction station which closed on 2 January 1922 can just be seen in the background.

What was once a rural area is fast becoming a suburb of Weston-super-Mare with much new housing, and to that end a new station has recently been opened at Worle. On September 1993 HST powercar No 43017 leads its train round the curve at Worle with a service to Paddington. *R. Poxon/Alan Cornish*

Uphill junction

To the west the Weston-super-Mare branch rejoins the main line at Uphill junction. The junction box can just be seen behind '4100' class 2-6-2T No 4143 as it heads westwards with a down goods from Bristol.

The junction was singled on 12 October 1969, and on 31 January 1972 the line from here to Weston was reduced to a single track; the signalbox was closed on the same date. The simplified junction can be seen as Class 47 No 47813 prepares to traverse the Weston branch with a service from Plymouth to Paddington (via Weston-super-Mare). *M. J. Fox/ Alan Cornish*

Weston-super-Mare General

Weston-super-Mare General in the 1920s. The station pictured here was not constructed until 1884 and is situated on a loop that runs to and from the main Bristol-Taunton line. The original terminus station at Locking Road was opened in 1841 and saw use in later years as an excursion station. The main buildings at Weston-super-Mare are now listed and in recent years have been refurbished, as seen on 17 August 1993 as Sprinter No 150249 waits to leave with a service to Birmingham New Street. *Real Photos /Author*

Weston-super-Mare (Locking Road)

The excursion station at Locking Road, seen here in August 1962 as 'King' class 4-6-0 No 6018 *King Henry VI* moves the empty stock for the 2.35pm service to Paddington round to Weston General. The small engine shed (closed August 1960) can be seen on the right; on the left a 'Grange' class 4-6-0 stands on the turntable. The station was closed to passengers on 6 September 1964 and today the site is used as a car and bus park.
G. F. Heiron/Alan Cornish

Bridgwater (Sedgmoor)
'Castle' class 4-6-0 No 5053 *Earl Cairns* arrives at Bridgwater (Sedgmoor) on 16 June 1959 with the 10.20am service from Taunton to Paddington. The station is still open and is seen here on 23 January 1994 as Sprinter No 150242 departs with the 11.32am service from Taunton to Bristol. The footbridge together with the main buildings have survived almost intact but at the time of writing the station is being modernised.
J. F. Loader/Peter Triggs

Ilminster
A 16-mile branch ran from Creech St Michael junction, east of Taunton, to Chard where it connected with the ex-LSWR branch from Chard Junction.

Ilminster was one of the small intermediate stations on the branch. The station is pictured here in the 1950s as a '7400' class 0-6-0PT No 7436 arrives with the 1.35pm service from Chard Central to Taunton. Ilminster was closed to passengers on 10 September 1962, but remained open for goods traffic until 6 July 1964. Both the station building and the goods shed are still extant and can be seen here on 5 August 1993 in industrial use.
R. E. Toop/Author

Bridgwater

'Castle' class 4-6-0 No 5090 *Neath Abbey* approaches Bridgwater station on 14 June 1959 with the 6.45pm service from Taunton to Bristol. Waiting in the up siding to attach a pair of open wagons to the rear of the train is 'Grange' class 4-6-0 No 6833 *Caldicot Grange*. This was apparently quite a regular working. Seen from the station footbridge in August 1993 an HST approaches the station with a service from Plymouth to Paddington. Notice the trackside hut on the right still *in situ*.
J. F. Loader/Alan Cornish

Chard Central
Chard Central, pictured here in the early 1960s, was opened as Chard Joint on 11 September 1866 being renamed Chard on 1 March 1928 and Chard Central on 11 March 1950. The station is seen to good effect as '7400' class 0-6-0PT No 7436 arrives with a passenger service from Taunton. Passenger services to Taunton were withdrawn on 10 September 1962. However the station remained open for services to Chard Junction until 7 March 1966. I am given to understand that the station building is now listed, and on 5 August 1993 was in use as a tyre depot.
David Lawrence/Author

Taunton
'Castle' class 4-6-0 No 7001 *Sir James Milne* stands at Taunton on 2 May 1959 with the RCTS Brunel Centenary special from Paddington to Saltash and Plymouth (Millbay).

Today the centre platform at Taunton is closed with part of the area planted with trees and shrubs. On 25 January 1994 a Regional Railways Class 158, No 158825, stands at the down platform with the 10.00am service from Cardiff to Paignton. Standing in the old Barnstaple departure bay (platform 3) is station pilot Class 08 No 08953.
Hugh Ballantyne/Peter Triggs

Norton Fitzwarren
The attractive station at Norton Fitzwarren in the 1920s. It was situated just west of Taunton and was the junction station for the branches to Minehead and Barnstaple. The station was closed on 30 October 1961, and the Barnstaple and Minehead branches closed on 3 October 1966 and 4 January 1971 respectively.

On 16 July 1993 a Class 158 unit No 158840 passes the site of Norton Fitzwarren station with a down Exeter service. The line on the right served the nearby Taunton Cider plant until the demise of BR's Speedlink freight service and provides a connection to the preserved West Somerset Railway.
Ian Allan Library/Author

Williton

A '4500' class 2-6-2T No 5571 arrives at Williton on 22 August 1961 with the 11am, service to Minehead. The scene is recreated, except for the footbridge (which was removed in 1971), in September 1993 as preserved '4100' class 2-6-2T No 4160 arrives with a Minehead service.
M. Hale/Alan Cornish

Watchet

The 11.12am service to Taunton hauled by '5700' class 0-6-0PT No 9764 arrives at Watchet on 22 August 1961. This was the original terminus of the line. It was opened by the Bristol & Exeter Railway on 31 March 1862 and was extended through to Minehead on 16 July 1874.

The station is seen here in September 1993 as '4100' class 2-6-2T No 4160 arrives with a service from Minehead to Bishops Lydeard.
M. Hale/Alan Cornish

Minehead

Minehead station is seen here in 1921; on the left is the small engine shed. Notice also the attractive station building. The second picture is taken from a slightly different angle on 7 April 1959 as a '5700' class 0-6-0PT No 9732 waits with a service to Taunton. The platform canopy was installed in 1934 when the platform was extended. The line closed to passengers on 4 January 1971 but was subsequently taken over and operated by the West Somerset Railway Society. Today the site of the old engine shed, which closed in December 1956, is a car park but the old goods shed still stands and is now used for locomotive restoration.
Real Photos/R. N. Joanes/Alan Cornish

Wellington

Wellington station pictured here on 15 November 1932. The original two track layout was extended during 1931 to give two through running lines and two platform loops. The Middle signalbox on the left was opened on 12 July 1931, and the new station on 21 February 1932.

Wellington was closed to passengers on 5 October 1964, the signalbox lasted somewhat longer being closed on 3 March 1986. The remains of the station are seen here on 26 January 1994 as an HST set powered by Nos 43029/43004 speeds through with the 11.35am service from Paddington to Plymouth.
GW Trust/Peter Triggs

Section 3
The Southwest

Devon and Cornwall

A selection of GWR publicity posters from the GW Trust's collection.

The counties of Devon and Cornwall were served by both the Great Western and the London & South Western Railways. On 30 December 1962 all of the ex-LSWR lines and branches in Devon and Cornwall were taken over by the Western Region. Between 1965 and 1970 much of the old LSWR system in Devon and Cornwall was closed leaving just the the main line from Waterloo to Exeter, and branches to Barnstaple, Exmouth and Gunnislake. At Launceston a short section of the line to Padstow is operated by the narrow gauge Launceston Steam Railway.

The Great Western fared slightly better, as the main line (although singled in places) has remained intact right through to Penzance. Branches are still open to St Ives and Newquay on the north coast and to Falmouth and Looe on the south, and the Lostwithiel-Fowey branch is still used for china clay traffic. There are also three preserved lines, the Bodmin & Wenford, the Paignton & Dartmouth Steam Railway, from Paignton to

Kingswear; and the South Devon Railway from Totnes to Buckfastleigh. The Plym Valley Railway has established its base at Marsh Mills on the old Plymouth-Yelverton line. On 12 May 1986 a new Parkway station was opened at Tiverton on the site of Sampford Peverell station and from that date the old station at Tiverton Junction was closed.

British Rail services in the southwest are today operated using HSTs and the new generation of diesel multiple-units. These are interspersed with a few Class 47 locomotive-hauled services. InterCity services between London, Plymouth and Penzance are operated almost exclusively using HST sets, although (particularly during the summer months) the occasional loco-motive-hauled service is added to the timetable. Intermediate services are operated by Regional Railways and are generally in the hands of Class 150, 153, 156 and 158 units. The ex-LSWR Waterloo-Exeter services are now operated by Network SouthEast using the newly-introduced Class 159s

(which are actually Class 158 'clones').

Branch line services in the two counties were until recently operated using 'Heritage' DMUs but these are now gradually being replaced by Class 150 and 153 units. Freight traffic in Devon and Cornwall now mainly comprises oil, fertilizer, stone and china clay, the services being operated using Class 37, 47, 56 and 60 locomotives. HST, locomotive and unit servicing for the area is now centred on Plymouth's Laira depot, although a refuelling and carriage servicing depot has been retained at Penzance.

In terms of passenger numbers the busiest of the remaining ex-Great Western branches is undoubtedly from St Erth to St Ives. It is particularly busy during the summer months, owing in no small measure to the park and ride station at Lelant Saltings. This was opened in 1978 as part of the St Ives park and ride scheme and without doubt has helped to ensure the future of this busy branch. Interestingly the St Ives branch, which opened on 1 June 1877, was the very last

line to be built using Brunel's 7ft 0¼in broad gauge.

The town of Falmouth is still a popular holiday destination and I have no doubt that this is partly due to the fact that it still has a railway. The branch which joins the main line at Truro was opened on 24 August 1864. At Falmouth a short spur served the nearby docks. During 1967 it seemed the line might close but instead the branch underwent a certain amount of rationalisation with all intermediate stations becoming unstaffed halts. On 6 May 1968 a new single platform station was opened at Falmouth. This was closer to the town centre than the old terminus station, the latter being closed on the same day. This did not prove to be a success and on 5 May 1975 a single platform was reopened at the old terminus which again became Falmouth. The 1968 station was renamed 'The Dell'. The rail connection to the docks is currently unused but for a number of years there has been talk of reinstating the connection to serve a new container port.

The Newquay branch was opened in stages between Fowey and Newquay by the Cornwall Mineral Railway in 1874. It was initially a goods-only line but on 20 June 1876 passenger services commenced between Fowey and Newquay. The branch was connected to the Great Western main line at Par on 1 January 1879 and it is from here that branch services are operated. The line which saw great usage during the holiday boom of the 1930s, 1940s and 1950s has now been run down to provide a basic railway. The regular DMU services from Par are supplemented, during the summer months, with weekend through services to and from Paddington.

The other remaining ex-Great Western branch is the line from Liskeard to Looe. The line was opened for passengers by the Liskeard & Looe Union Canal Co between Moorswater, where it connected with the earlier Liskeard & Caradon Railway Co, and Looe on 11 September 1879. The line was extended from Moorswater to Liskeard where it connected with the Great Western main line on 25 February 1901. At Liskeard a small terminus station was constructed. This stood at right angles to the Great Western station and was opened for passenger traffic on 15 May 1901, and is still in use today. The branch is particularly interesting as trains still have to reverse direction at Coombe junction, at the bottom of the fierce climb to Liskeard and at the point of connection to the Moorswater line, where the canal arch is still visible.

Burlescombe
Burlescombe stood on the Great Western main line just to the west of Whiteball Tunnel. On 2 July 1955 'Hall' class No 6946 *Heatherden Hall* rushes past with the 9.10am service from Liverpool to Plymouth. The station was closed on 5 October 1964 and there is little evidence left on 5 August 1993 as Class 47 No 47839 rushes through with a down West of England service.
R. C. Riley/Author

Dulverton

Dulverton was an important intermediate station on the Taunton-Barnstaple line as it was also the junction station for the branch to Tiverton and Exeter. The branch joined the Barnstaple line to the east of the station, at Morebath junction. The Tiverton branch was closed on 7 October 1963. The Taunton-Barnstaple line remained open until 3 October 1966. The station buildings and goods shed are still intact and are now used for staff accommodation by the nearby hotel, with part of the trackbed now a tennis court. 4 August 1993. *R. C. Riley/Author*

Bampton

This picture shows one of the intermediate stations on the Dulverton-Tiverton branch, at Bampton (Devon) where on 26 February 1960 0-6-0PT No 7761 arrives with the 1.35pm service from Dulverton to Exeter. As already mentioned, the branch closed on 7 October 1963; since then the site has been levelled and is now used as a car park and a children's play area. The old road bridge although not now used is still *in situ* just behind the trees. *J. Spencer-Gilks/Author*

Hemyock

A popular line with photographers was the branch from Tiverton Junction to Hemyock. It was operated for many years by ex-GW '4800' class 0-4-2Ts with an ex-Barry Railway coach. In this picture 0-4-2T No 1420 together with the ex-Barry coach is seen taking water at Hemyock in the early 1960s. The line was closed to passenger traffic on 9 September 1963 but remained open to serve the St Ivel creamery until 31 October 1975. Today the site has been taken over by the creamery and large storage tanks now occupy the position of the station. 5 August 1993. *Ian Allan Library/Author*

Culmstock
Culmstock was one of two intermediate stations on the branch. It is pictured here on 22 June 1963 as 0-4-2T No 1450 departs with the 9.20am (SO) from Tiverton Junction. The site is now a children's playground and a car park for the adjacent 'Culm Valley' pub.
G. D. King/Author

Tiverton Junction
The branch joined the main line at Tiverton Junction. The station is seen here on 28 January 1932, shortly before reconstruction. The overall roof bay platform on the left was for services to and from Tiverton. The Hemyock bay is on the right. The new station was opened in October of the same year and is seen here on 24 February 1962 as '4800' class 0-4-2T No 1462 shunts some milk tanks that it has just conveyed from Hemyock. The signalbox on the up platform was closed on 3 March 1986. The station itself was closed on 12 May 1986 when a new station, Tiverton Parkway, was opened on the site of Sampford Peverell Halt (closed 5 October 1964). On 25 January 1994 an HST speeds through the remains of Tiverton Junction with the 7.20am service from Penzance to Edinburgh (the 'Cornish Scot'). Notice that the platform loops are still *in situ*.
GW Trust/Ian Allan Library/Peter Triggs

Tiverton Town

'4800' class 0-4-2T No 1450 waits to depart from Tiverton Town station on 17 July 1964 with the auto-service to Tiverton Junction. The station which stood on the Exeter to Dulverton branch was closed on 5 October 1964 with the withdrawal of services to Tiverton Junction. As already mentioned, the Exeter-Dulverton branch was closed on 7 October 1963. After closure the station was demolished and the site lay derelict until during the last year when a new inner relief road, pictured here on 25 January 1994, was constructed on the disused trackbed.
D. C. Smith/Peter Triggs

Silverton

Silverton was situated on the Great Western main line to the northeast of Exeter. The station had staggered platforms, and the picture here shows the up platform (the down platform being situated behind the photographer) as 'Hall' class No 5967 *Bickmarsh Hall* speeds through with a westbound parcels train. The small signalbox was actually closed on 21 November 1928 but was retained for use as a store. Silverton was closed to passengers on 5 October 1964. Today the site is marked by milepost 186¾ — otherwise there is little remaining although some fencing can still be seen on the left.
R. C. Riley/Amyas Crump

Cowley Bridge junction

Ex-Great Western '4700' class 2-8-0 No 4708 coasts past Cowley Bridge junction, Exeter, on 25 July 1953 with the 1.25pm service from Paddington to Kingswear. Diverging away to the left is the ex-LSWR route to Barnstaple and Plymouth. The ex-LSWR line was singled on 17 December 1984 and Cowley Bridge Junction signalbox was closed on 1 March 1985. Looking down from the same spot on 25 January 1994 the 9.35am Paddington to Plymouth HST speeds past the junction. The interesting building on the right is the Cowley Bridge Inn.
D. Trevor Rowe/Peter Triggs

Exeter St Davids

A down relief service from the Midlands to Torquay and Paignton pulls out of Exeter St Davids in September 1963 behind 'Hall' class 4-6-0 No 5992 *Horton Hall*. At this time Great Western main line services used platforms 1 and 2 with ex-LSWR services from Waterloo using 3 and 4. This has now changed and today these services have switched platforms. On 21 August 1993 Class 159 No 159016 waits at platform 1 with a service to Waterloo. In recent years the ornate façade above platform 1 has been replaced by some rather plain cladding.
J. B. Mounsey/Amyas Crump

Exeter St Davids

'Castle' class No 5052 *Earl of Radnor* passes the large Exeter West signalbox as it arrives at Exeter on 1 September 1957 with a Penzance-Paddington service. On the left is the ex-LSWR route to Exeter Central and Waterloo. The signalbox was closed on 3 May 1985 and has since been preserved, at Crewe. Seen from the same spot on 21 August 1993, Class 159 No 159015 arrives with a service from Waterloo. Interestingly Exeter is now the only station in England where trains to and from London regularly arrive and depart in both directions.
J. C. Way/Amyas Crump

Exminster

An early view of the station at Exminster looking east. The station was enlarged to four platforms in June 1924. Notice the water tank on the up platform; I wonder how often it was used as there were watertroughs nearby. The station closed to passengers on 30 March 1964. The Great Western is still in evidence in the form of the stationmaster's house and the signalbox which was built in 1924 and closed in 1985. It is now used as an observation point for the local nature conservancy.
Real Photos/Amyas Crump

Dawlish

The small footbridge at the east end of Dawlish provides a fine vantage point as 'Hall' class 4-6-0 No 6932 *Burwarton Hall* departs on 4 July 1953 with the 5.45pm service to Exeter. The beach seems strangely deserted: perhaps all the holidaymakers have left for their hotels and evening dinner.

On 9 August 1993 Sprinter No 150242 departs with a service from Paignton to Exmouth. The small goods yard on the right was closed in 1965 and is now the station car park. Because of its close proximity to the sea, the line at this point has been damaged on several occasions by winter storms.
K. Wells/Author

Dawlish

As can be seen from the previous pictures, between Newton Abbot and Exeter, the main line skirts the coast. Looking down from the footbridge at Dawlish in June 1959, 'King' class 4-6-0 No 6003 *King George IV* emerges from Parsons Tunnel and runs through the station with a Plymouth-Paddington service.

On 9 August 1993 an unidentified HST accelerates through the station with the modern-day service from Plymouth to Paddington. *D. Sellman/Author*

Teignmouth
An up goods hauled by ex-Great Western '2884' class 2-8-0 No 3834 runs through Teignmouth on 8 August 1956. This photogenic location has been used over the years by many generations of photographers.

Apart from the absence of signals, the spot has changed little as Class 158 No 158816 leaves the station on 9 August 1993 with a service to Exeter. *T. E. Williams/ Author*

Newton Abbot

I suppose that you could say that these three pictures illustrate the rise and fall of Newton Abbot. The first picture shows Newton Abbot in around 1920. Notice that the station at this time was much smaller with an overall roof. This was removed when the station was reconstructed and enlarged during 1926/7. The old West box (left) was closed on 3 April 1927. It is difficult nowadays to envisage just how busy Newton Abbot once was. During its heyday it was possibly the busiest station in the southwest. Some idea can be gleaned from the photograph below taken on a Saturday afternoon in July 1957 with locomotives and stock occupying almost every track. On view are two 'Castles', a 'Britannia', 'Hall', 'Manor' and a '9400' pannier.

Newton Abbot is now a pale shadow of itself as can be seen in this shot taken on a rainy Saturday in July 1993. A solitary HST waits in the platform with the 9am service to London. The busy locomotive depot on the right in picture 2 was closed to steam on 1 April 1962 and to diesels in May 1973. The 'new' West box seen in the second picture was closed on 2 May 1987 and during the same month the station was reduced to just three platforms, with the down relief platform and bays being converted into a large car park. The derelict locomotive works and diesel depot can be seen in the centre right of this view *GW Trust/D. S. Fish/Author*

Heathfield

The branch from Newton Abbot to Moretonhampstead was opened by the South Devon Railway on 4 July 1866. It was closed to passengers on 2 March 1959 and to goods on 6 April 1964.

Heathfield was an important station on the branch as it was the junction for the branch to Chudleigh and Exeter (closed to passengers on 9 June 1958 and to freight in stages between 1961 and 1968). In this picture 0-6-0PT No 3659 stands at Heathfield station on 17 April 1959. The signalbox which controlled the junction and the small yard closed on 12 October 1965.

After 1964 the southern part of the line remained open as far as Heathfield to serve an oil depot. Today the track is still *in situ*, as seen in this picture taken on 10 September 1993.
Dr Geoff Smith/Author

Bovey Tracey

Another intermediate station on the branch was at Bovey Tracey, seen here on 17 April 1959 and just a month after closure to passengers. An ex-Great Western '5700' class 0-6-0PT No 3659 still provides some interest as it shunts the pick-up freight.

Incredibly most of the buildings including the goods shed survive although the trackbed now forms part of the main road from Bovey to Moretonhampstead.
Dr Geoff Smith/Author

Moretonhampstead

The terminus at Moretonhampstead is pictured here on 26 September 1958. Ex-Great Western 0-6-0PT No 9678 waits at the single platform with the 3.15pm service to Newton Abbot.

The station site is now used by a transport company with many of the original buildings being retained for further use. In the centre is the large goods shed and in the left background the train shed roof can just be seen.
Ian Allan Library/Author

Moretonhampstead
The small engine shed at Moretonhampstead was closed on 28 November 1947 but was in use in this 1950s shot for storing coal. Notice the small signalbox at the side of the shed.

The shed is still very much intact and on 10 September 1993 was being used as a servicing bay for the company's tractor units.
Ian Allan Library/Author

Kingskerswell
Kingskerswell was the first station on the Torquay and Kingswear line. At the time of the photo (1921) the station served a small population, but in recent years the village has expanded with much new housing. Unfortunately this came too late to save the station which had closed on 5 October 1964. On 11 August 1993 both platforms remain as does the entrance footpath on the right. *Real Photos/Amyas Crump*

Torre

Torre station pictured here in 1921. The station is situated on the stiff climb from Torquay up to Newton Abbot.

The second shot was taken on 8 August 1993 and shows how little the station has changed. The large goods shed seen in the first picture remains. Today Torre is an unstaffed halt with the main entrance building in current use as an antiques shop.
Ian Allan Library/Author

Torquay

These three shots are divided by just over 100 years and show the east end of Torquay station. The line was opened between Newton Abbot and Torquay by the South Devon Railway on 18 December 1848. The first picture was taken in April 1892 and shows the old broad gauge layout, the second view was taken from the same location in 1921 and the third in August 1993. Apart from the removal of the centre track (1965) and of the two sidings on the right (1970) the station has seen little change.
Real Photos (2)/Author

Torquay

I have included these two pictures of the west end of Torquay station to show the preserved signalbox on the down platform. This box which is apparently listed along with the station was closed on 15 November 1984.

It is seen in working condition in June 1958 as a 'Hall' class 4-6-0 No 7929 *Wyke Hall* arrives with the down 'Devonian', the 9.5am service from Bradford to Paignton.

The closed, but preserved, box can be seen to good effect in this picture taken on 8 August 1993 of Class 159 No 159012 arriving with a through Waterloo-Paignton service. *N. Brayshaw/Author*

Paignton

I wonder just how many millions of holiday-makers have arrived and departed from Paignton over the years. The station is pictured here in about 1921 and just prior to the construction of the new down-side bay. Looking down from approximately the same spot on 29 September 1993, a Class 158 No 158871 waits at the up platform with a service to Bristol. The down bay platform and yard were taken over by the Dart Valley Railway on 1 November 1972 and today form a separate part of the station. The steam locomotive on the left is restored ex-Great Western 'Hall' No 4920 *Dumbleton Hall*.
Real Photos/Amyas Crump

Goodrington

'King' class No 6018 *King Henry VI* enters the carriage sidings at Goodrington on 21 July 1962 with empty carriage stock from Paignton. These sidings together with the adjacent goods shed were opened in July/August 1930.

The sidings here are still currently in use as can be seen in this shot taken in July 1993, but the goods yard which was closed in 1969 has since been covered with housing. Goodrington signalbox, seen on both pictures, was closed on 1 November 1972. The line on the far left is the privately-owned Paignton & Dartmouth Railway.
Ian Allan Library/Author

Goodrington Sands Halt

A view of Goodrington Sands Halt on 12 July 1962. 'Hall' class 4-6-0 No 4992 *Crosby Hall* pauses with a Kingswear-Manchester service whilst in the down platform a Class 22 diesel-hydraulic No D6332 waits with some empty stock. Also in shot is 'Hall' No 4978 *Westwood Hall*. The 'new' carriage sidings on the right were installed by the Western Region in June 1957.

In recent years a large water activity centre has been built adjacent to the station. This means that during the summer months a considerable number of passengers use the station. The 'new' sidings on the right although still *in situ* are now out of use.
Author's Collection/Author

Churston

Churston station on 18 August 1961. Just arrived at the down platform is the 1.36pm service from Kingswear to Paddington hauled by 'Hall' 4-6-0 No 4984 *Albrighton Hall*. Standing in the bay is a two-car DMU with the 2.20pm service to Brixham. The Brixham branch was closed on 13 May 1963 (just before the summer season and its busiest time!).

The Paignton & Dartmouth Railway have in recent years completely restored the station and have constructed new repair shops. On 8 August 1993 the service was being worked by ex-LNER 'A3' Pacific No 60103 *Flying Scotsman*, while on the right outside the repair shops is preserved ex-BR Class 03 No D2192.
Ian Allan Library/Author

Kingswear

Kingswear is the terminus of the Paignton-Dartmouth line. These three pictures date from 1921 to 1993 and illustrate how little Kingswear (and Dartmouth across the river) have changed over the years. This first picture was taken in 1921 and shows to good effect the small dock and coal wharves. These lasted until the 1950s but then fell out of use.

A few of the coal sidings remain in the second shot, taken in September 1953, of 'Hall' class No 4992 *Crosby Hall* departing with a service to Birmingham Snow Hill.

The third picture was taken on 8 August 1993 and shows ex-LNER 4-6-2 No 60103 *Flying Scotsman* arriving with a service from Paignton. The locomotive was newly painted in BR green livery and restored back to its 1960s condition and on loan to the railway for part of the summer season.
Ian Allan Library/J. Larkin/Author

Dartmouth

Although it was never physically connected to any railway Dartmouth boasted its own station. Rail tickets were issued here to all parts of the country but the nearest railway was across the River Dart at Kingswear, this being reached by ferry. The trainless 'station' at Dartmouth is seen here in the early 1940s. Ticketing facilities were withdrawn by the Western Region in 1964 and today the building is in use as a restaurant.
H. C. Casserley/Author

Totnes

Totnes station can just be seen in the background as a down goods service hauled by 2-6-2T No 4165 and 'Hall' 4-6-0 No 4991 *Cobham Hall* start the climb over Rattery Bank.

Over the years the undergrowth has started to creep in but luckily the shot is still repeatable as Class 158 No 158820 starts its ascent of the bank with a through service from Bath to Penzance on 8 August 1993.
R. E. Toop/Author

Ashburton

A short branch ran from Totnes and along the Dart valley up to Ashburton. The line was opened by the South Devon Railway on 1 May 1872. It was closed to passengers on 3 November 1958 and to goods on 10 September 1962 but was taken over and operated by the Dart Valley Railway from 5 April 1969.

The terminus at Ashburton is pictured here on 2 July 1957 and shows 0-4-2T No 1427 with a service to Totnes. The section between Ashburton and Buckfastleigh was unfortunately abandoned to allow for road improvements. Since then the station building at Ashburton has seen further use as a garage and with the end wall blocked up this is the only shot possible of the old train shed. Although not pictured, the old steam shed is still *in situ*. 5 September 1993.
R. C. Riley/Author

Buckfastleigh

The main station and terminus on what is now the 'South Devon Railway' is at Buckfastleigh. In this first shot taken on the 15 February 1958 '4800' class 0-4-2T No 1427, together with brake 3rd No M2067M, prepares to depart with the 2.45pm (SO) service from Ashburton to Totnes.

On 5 September 1993 the station has seen some change, notably the extension to the platform and the addition of a large cafeteria and shop (behind the station running-in board). *Hugh Ballantyne/Author*

Brent

Situated between Plymouth and Newton Abbot was the junction station at Brent. Here main line passengers changed for the Kingsbridge branch. On 17 July 1956 the branch train stands in the bay platform hauled by 0-6-0PT No 3796. On the main line 'Hall' class 4-6-0 No 4998 *Eydon Hall* pauses with the 7.55am service from Penzance to Swansea.

The Kingsbridge branch, which had opened on 19 December 1893, was closed on 16 September 1963. Brent station was itself closed on 5 October 1964.

On 8 August 1993 an HST speeds through Brent with the 9.00am Plymouth-Paddington service. The signalbox seen in both shots was closed on 17 October 1973, but the building has been retained for permanent way use.
R. J. Doran/Author

Kingsbridge

The terminus of the branch at Kingsbridge pictured here in the summer of 1956. '4500' class 2-6-2T No 5557 waits to depart with a service to Brent. The branch was particularly busy during the summer season and at peak times both platforms would be used. Part of the branch engine shed, which closed in September 1961, can just be seen on the right. In November 1963 the branch was the subject of a preservation appeal, but unfortunately this was unsuccessful.

Today it is impossible to get the same angle but this view shows the station building still *in situ* on 6 September 1993. The station site is now used for industrial purposes

with the main part being used as a bus garage.
D. A. Bosomworth/Author

Marsh Mills
The 2.5pm service from Launceston to Plymouth hauled by '4500' class 2-6-2T No 5532 pauses at Marsh Mills on 8 July 1961. The station was situated just to the east of Plymouth and on the line to Launceston.

The Launceston line closed on 31 December 1962 but the track at this point was retained to serve some private sidings. The signalbox was closed on 4 April 1965 and the remains of the platforms were removed soon after. The site of the old station has changed somewhat but today Marsh Mills is the headquarters of the Plym Valley Railway preservation group.
R. C. Riley/Dane Garrod

Tavistock South
Tavistock South was an important intermediate station on the Plymouth-Launceston line. The town was also served by the LSWR that ran into its own station at Tavistock North. On 16 April 1960 '4500' class 2-6-2T No 4549 arrives at Tavistock South with the 12.40pm service to Plymouth. South station was closed to passengers on 31 December 1962; North survived until 6 May 1968. With the closure of the GW station part of the site was used to form a new road. Looking from approximately the same spot but at a much lower level in August 1993 almost nothing remains of the railway, the main reference point being part of the abutments of the old road underbridge (above the gap in the hedge) seen on the left of the first picture.
J. C. Haydon/Author

Princetown

One of the more remote Great Western branches ran from the Launceston line at Yelverton to Princetown, high on Dartmoor. The branch for many years served the nearby prison as well as the small community here. The layout of the terminus at Princetown is well illustrated in this shot of '4400' class 2-6-2T No 4410 on a Caravan Club special on 17 April 1954.

The branch was closed on 5 March 1956 and today only the houses on the left mark the spot, but part of the old stable block remains and can just be seen centre right.
B. A. Butt/Author

Laira junction

This view of 'Grange' class 4-6-0 No 6873 *Caradoc Grange* passing Laira junction on a down freight was taken on 30 August 1961. The track diverging away to the right ran down to Friary junction. Laira Junction signalbox (right) was closed on 10 November 1973.

Today the high vantage point has gone but the background remains relatively unchanged as an HST service from London to Penzance approaches Plymouth in August 1993. The line on the right now provides access to Laira diesel and HST depot.
R. C. Riley/Clive Turner

Plymouth

'Castle' class No 5098 *Clifford Castle* makes a fine sight as it departs from Plymouth on 3 September 1963 with the 2pm service from Plymouth to Manchester. Apart from some track rationalisation it is amazing just how little has changed as an HST departs on 29 December 1993 with the 11.45am service from Penzance to Bristol Temple Meads.
J. S. Whiteley/Dane Garrod

Plymouth North Road

A view of Plymouth North Road station looking east on 27 February 1928. The station at this time comprised two covered train sheds which can be seen on the above photo. The station was partially reconstructed in 1939 when the up-side roof was removed but World War 2 curtailed further work and the rebuilding was not finally completed until 26 March 1962.

This picture of Class 150 No 150241 on a service to Gunnislake was taken from approximately the same spot on the now-extended down platform on 6 September 1993.
GW Trust/Author

Royal Albert Bridge

Ex-Great Western 2-8-0 No 3838 crosses Brunel's Royal Albert Bridge on 7 September 1962 with an up PW train. In the background the newly constructed road bridge rather overpowers the 1859 structure. The Royal Albert Bridge box on the right was closed on 28 June 1973.

There has always been restricted-speed single line working across the bridge, but the single line is now extended towards Plymouth as the original down line has been lifted. On 16 July 1993 Class 37 No 37671 approaches the now closed signalbox *en route* to Laira. *GW Trust /Author*

Saltash

Saltash is the first (or last, depending in which direction you are travelling) Great Western station in Cornwall. As can be seen it is situated just on the Cornish side of the Saltash Bridge. In July 1958 a 'Grange' class 4-6-0 No 6821 *Leaton Grange* and an unidentified 'Hall' approach Saltash station with the down 'Cornish Riviera Express'.

The station is still open, although now unstaffed. On 16 July 1993 Class 47 No 47848 enters the Duchy with the 12.35pm service from Paddington to Penzance. *D. Sellman/Author*

Liskeard

An ex-Great Western 2-6-2T No 4523 shunts the Moorswater goods at Liskeard station on 24 June 1955. The junction to the Liskeard-Looe branch can be seen to the left of the last wagon.

The same viewpoint on 12 August 1993 shows Class 158 No 158839 arriving with the 7.50am service from Bristol Temple Meads. Although the down-side buildings have been removed, the small shelter on the up platform still survives. *R. E. Vincent/Dane Garrod*

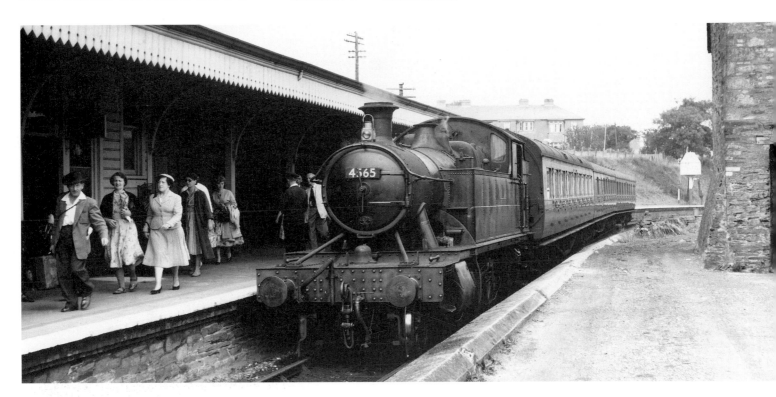

Liskeard

The branch from Liskeard to Looe was opened for passenger traffic on 15 May 1901. The single platform branch station at Liskeard stands at right angles to the main line station. It is seen here in August 1959 soon after the arrival of an afternoon service from Looe hauled by '4500' class 2-6-2T No 4565.

On 12 August 1993 a 'Heritage' DMU set No 842 arrives at the station with the 10.15am service from Looe. As can be seen, the station has recently been refurbished.
G. Bannister/Dane Garrod

Coombe junction

The imposing structure of Moorswater Viaduct can be seen in the background as 2-6-2T No 4526 leaves Coombe junction and starts its 2-mile climb up to Liskeard station with a service from Looe.

During the 1960s the branch was rationalised and today the simplified track layout at Coombe junction can be seen as 'Heritage' unit No 53314 approaches the station with the 10.55am service to Looe. All four intermediate stations on the branch now operate on a 'stop by request' basis.
R. C. Sambourne/Dane Garrod

Looe

The terminus of the branch at Looe is pictured here on 10 October 1953 and after the arrival of the 2.52pm service from Liskeard hauled by 2-6-2T No 4568. At one time this station boasted what was probably the smallest signalbox in the country, the six lever ground frame being housed in what can best be described as a tin hut. This was situated at rail level at the south end of the platform; interestingly although the hut was only large enough to house the ground frame it was fitted with a Great Western cast iron sign proclaiming 'Looe Signalbox'.

The terminus on 12 August 1993 as unit No L842 arrives with the 12.25pm service from Liskeard. The branch at this point has been cut back and the platform shortened with local police buildings now occupying part of the site. Notice that some wag has removed the 'E' from the station name — I hope that foreign tourists do not take it too literally!
Ian Allan Library/Dane Garrod

Menheniot
'Grange' class No 6801 *Aylburton Grange* runs through Menheniot station on 16 July 1956 with the 12.20pm Penzance-Kensington milk train. The sidings and goods loop on the left were removed during 1973. The station has now been reduced to an unstaffed halt.

Looking down from the station footbridge on 12 August 1993: Class 158 No 158820 approaches the rather overgrown up platform with the 10.25pm Penzance-Bath Spa service.
R. C. Riley/Dane Garrod

Par

An unidentified ex-Great Western '5700' class 0-6-0PT moves a long freight from the Newquay branch through the small yard at Par in the 1950s. The Par-Newquay branch was opened for goods traffic on 1 June 1874 and for passenger traffic on 20 June 1876. During 1872 the Great Western opened an unusual half roundhouse locomotive shed, a short distance away at St Blazey. The shed, which is still *in situ* and listed, continued to be used as a stabling point until April 1987. Today locomotives stable in the yard nearby.

On 11 August 1993 Class 37 No 37673 runs through the station at Par *en route* to the stabling point at St Blazey. *B. A. Butt/Dane Garrod*

Par
The west end of Par station with 'County' class No 1002 *County of Berks* arriving with the up 'Cornishman' on 18 May 1959. Par is the junction station for the branch to Newquay which can be seen diverging away to the right. The water tank has gone but otherwise there is little change apart from motive power as an HST arrives on 11 August 1993 with the 9.42am service from Penzance to Paddington. At the time of writing the signalbox, seen in both views, is still operational.
M. Mensing/Dane Garrod

Quintrel Downs

Ex-Great Western '4500' class 2-6-2T No 4559 with the 2.40pm service to Newquay stands at Quintrel Downs on the Newquay-Par branch in the 1950s. The small ground frame hut on the right controlled the adjacent level crossing.

Amazingly the station is still open and is seen here on 12 August 1993 as Class 153 units Nos 153370/153355 pause with the 3.21pm service to Newquay. The two sidings seen in the first picture were removed in January 1965. *D. Kelk/Dane Garrod*

Newquay

The branch terminates at Newquay. The town was at one time an important port for the export of china clay. By the turn of the century this traffic had declined and over the ensuing years the town gained importance as Cornwall's premier holiday centre. The first picture shows the station in the early 1920s; the gradual increase in holiday trade resulted in the Great Western enlarging the station on no less than three separate occasions between 1928 and 1938. However, the decline in passenger traffic during the 1960s and early 1970s saw many of the facilities withdrawn. The exclusive use of DMUs on services to Newquay has seen the removal of run around facilities and today only a single platform is in use. 12 August 1993.
Ian Allan Library/Dane Garrod

Goonbell Halt

This pair of shots illustrate just how the railway can completely disappear. Goonbell Halt stood on the Chacewater-Newquay branch. It is seen here in the 1950s as a '4500' class 2-6-2T No 5500 arrives with a service from Newquay to Truro. The branch closed on 4 February 1963 and from this picture you would have some difficulty being persuaded that there once was a railway here, the only reference point being the line of trees in the background.

Part of the Chacewater-Newquay route can still be travelled over by courtesy of the 15in gauge Lappa Valley Railway.

G. Clarke/Dane Garrod

Falmouth

The rather impressive station at Falmouth seen here on 25 September 1951 as 2-6-2T No 5526 stands under the overall roof after arriving with the 9.9am service from Truro. Fellow class member No 5515 waits at the up platform with the 9.55am service to Truro. The branch was opened by the Cornwall Railway on 24 August 1863, being absorbed by the Great Western in 1889.

The overall roof was removed in the early 1950s and replaced by the canopy seen in the second picture. During the late 1960s and early 1970s the branch was extensively rationalised. At the Falmouth end a new single platform station was opened nearer the town on 7 December 1970 and from that date the old station was closed and partially removed. The old down platform seen in the first picture was reopened for passenger traffic on 5 May 1975 as Falmouth, when the 1970 platform was renamed 'The Dell'. Today all stations on the branch are unstaffed halts. *H. Bowtell/Dane Garrod*

Chacewater

'Castle' class No 4095 *Harlech Castle* approaches Chacewater station on 16 May 1959 with the 6.20am Penzance-Kensington milk train. The bay platform on the left was used by services to Perranporth and Newquay. These were withdrawn when the branch closed on 4 February 1963.

Chacewater was closed on 5 October 1964, although the signalbox on the down platform survived until 12 June 1973. The old down platform still survives and can just be seen in this shot of HST power car No 43065 as it speeds by with a through service to the northeast on 10 August 1993.
M. Mensing/Dane Garrod

Camborne

Looking down from the footbridge at Camborne in July 1950 the photographer has captured ex-Great Western 0-6-0PT No 7422 passing through the station on shunting duties. The goods shed (top left) and yard here were situated on the down side. The yard was closed in 1965 and has since been built on. In this view of the station in August 1993 the up-side building remains although now devoid of its canopy as Class 158 No 158825 arrives with the 10.25am service from Penzance to Bath Spa.
G. Clarke/Dane Garrod

Gwinear Road

Gwinear Road station looking west in 1920. From 9 May 1887 Gwinear Road became the junction for Helston branch services. The bay platform can be seen on the left. Gwinear Road was closed on 5 October 1964, the same day as the Helston branch. Today only the remains of the down platform remain and when this is removed only milepost 316 will mark the site.
Ian Allan Library/Dane Garrod

Helston

The Helston branch was opened on 9 May 1887 and, as already mentioned, ran from the Great Western main line at Gwinear Road to the single platform terminus station at Helston, pictured here in 1910. In the centre, beyond the platform, the engine shed can just be seen; this was closed in December 1963. The branch itself did not last much longer, being closed on 5 October 1964.

The second picture taken on 6 August 1993 shows the approximate site of Helston station. This view was chosen as it shows the old goods shed (left centre) which is all that is left of the railway here and now forms part of a new flats complex. It was actually situated just to the right of the first picture.
Ian Allan Library/Dane Garrod

Hayle Viaduct

'County' class No 1015 *County of Gloucester* crosses the 308yd-long Hayle Viaduct with a down Plymouth-Penzance stopping service in the late 1950s. The original wooden viaduct, which was designed by Brunel, was constructed in 1852. It was replaced by the stone structure seen here in 1883, the line being doubled over the viaduct in 1899.

The second picture shows the viaduct on 6 August 1993. The station is still open but is now an unstaffed halt. Interestingly the storehouse of the local brewery (left in the first view) has now gone but parked on the adjacent road is a delivery vehicle advertising a well known Australian lager. *J. C. Beckett/Dane Garrod*

St Erth

St Erth station on 19 April 1952. This was and still is the junction station for the branch to St Ives. The branch train hauled by an ex-Great Western 2-6-2T No 4566 stands in the bay platform whilst 'Britannia' 4-6-2 No 70019 *Lightning* arrives with the up 'Cornish Riviera' service.

   St Erth photographed from the East signalbox on 6 August 1993 as the Penzance-St Ives service, formed of a 'Heritage' DMU, prepares to leave the up platform and cross over to the branch. The station itself has actually changed little.

B. A. Butt/Dane Garrod

St Ives

The St Ives branch was one of the more scenic of the West Country branch lines. The branch which opened in 1 June 1877 was the very last to be built using Brunel's 7ft 0¼in gauge. The Great Western's 'Holiday Line' tag is well illustrated in this view which shows a portion of the down 'Cornish Riviera' service hauled by a '4500' class 2-6-2T arriving at St Ives on 1 August 1953. Notice, centre right, the small engine shed and of course on the left the rather crowded sandy beach.

Some 40 years later on 13 August 1993 the beach is less crowded and the old station area is now a car park. The replacement single concrete platform, seen centre right, was opened on 21 May 1971.

B. A. Butt/Dane Garrod

Marazion

'Grange' class No 6837 *Forthampton Grange* pulls out of Marazion station on 23 September 1959 with the 12 noon service from Penzance to Plymouth. The two coaches next to the locomotive are through coaches to Glasgow. Notice also the camping coach on the left.

Marazion was closed to passengers on 5 October 1964. On 6 August 1993 only the downside building remains, but the Great Western camping coach tradition continues with the six ex-Pullman camping coaches.
P. Treloar/Dane Garrod

Long Rock, Penzance

'Grange' class No 6875 *Hindford Grange* with the 1.55pm Penzance-Plymouth passes the ex-Great Western Locomotive depot at Long Rock, Penzance, on 11 May 1959. The depot was closed to steam on 10 September 1962 but continued to be used as a diesel depot until 1976; it was demolished during the same year to make way for a new HST and carriage servicing depot. The same spot on 6 August 1993 shows part of the locomotive and carriage servicing facility. The main line here was singled in June 1974.
M. Mensing/Dane Garrod

Penzance

The station at Penzance was opened by the West Cornwall Railway on 11 March 1852. The original single platform station is seen here in mixed gauge days. The large building on the left is the goods shed and alongside is what appears to be a single road engine shed. The old station was rebuilt during November 1880 to provide an extra platform and a larger overall roof. The revised layout is seen here in the 1920s. Notice that the 'engine' shed has now become part of the goods depot.

In 1939 the station was once again enlarged to give a four platform formation as seen in the top picture overleaf taken in the 1950s which shows 'Grange' class No 6826 *Nannerth Grange* leaving with a parcels train.

The present layout at Penzance is seen in the lower picture on 6 August 1993, the only occupant being a Class 08 pilot. The station has undergone some refurbishment in the last couple of years including replacement of the overall roof. *GW Trust/Real Photos/J. Davenport/Dane Garrod*

Section 4
The Midlands, Cotswolds and Border Counties

Gloucester, Shropshire, Warwickshire, The West Midlands, Hereford & Worcester

A selection of GWR publicity posters from the GW Trust's collection.

In years gone by the main line between Paddington and Birkenhead formed an important part of the Great Western system. Unfortunately the days of through services between Paddington, Wolverhampton and Birkenhead are long gone and, although much of the old route still remains, most of it has been downgraded, now being operated by a number of different sectors. The cut-off route between Princes Risborough and Aynho junction, which was opened by the Great Western in 1910, has now been singled and is served by Network SouthEast 'Chiltern Line' services. Today main line services from Paddington to Birmingham and beyond are operated by InterCity and run via Oxford. At Leamington they diverge from the old Great Western route and take the ex-London & North Western Railway branch to Coventry. The section between Leamington and the new station at Birmingham Snow Hill is now operated by Regional Railways and Centro (West Midlands PTE). The ex-Great Western

main line between Snow Hill and Wolverhampton Low Level was closed in March 1972. Therefore to bridge the gap today one has to leave Snow Hill and cross the city to New Street and travel via the ex-L&NWR line to Wolverhampton High Level. Services between here and Shrewsbury are again operated by Centro. From Shrewsbury to Chester and from Chester to Hooton services are operated by Regional Railways. Between Hooton and Birkenhead Central (the Great Western & Birkenhead Joint station at Birkenhead Woodside was closed on 5 November 1967) the line is electrified and operated by Merseyrail EMUs.

Ex-Great Western lines in the Birmingham area have in recent years seen considerable investment in new rolling-stock, along with the construction of new stations at Moor Street and Snow Hill. Currently there are plans to extend the line northwards through to Smethwick West where it will link up with the Kidderminster line. At the present time services from

Great Malvern and Worcester run into New Street but with the completion of the new link will once again arrive at Snow Hill. Suburban services over ex-Great Western lines in the Birmingham area are now generally operated using Class 150 Sprinter units, although a few 'Heritage' DMUs still survive. These services are supplemented over certain routes by Regional Railways Class 158 and Thames & Chiltern Class 165/166 units. InterCity trains from the Oxford line to Birmingham and beyond are now operated using either Class 47s or HSTs.

The Midlands steam enthusiast is well catered for with a number of ex-Great Western lines being operated by railway preservation societies. The Severn Valley Railway operates passenger services from its own station at Kidderminster through to Bridgnorth, over the remains of the old Great Western route to Shrewsbury. Further south the Gloucestershire & Warwickshire Railway currently operate seasonal services between Toddington and Winchcombe

over part of the Stratford-on-Avon to Cheltenham line, with the eventual intention of opening through to Cheltenham. The Dean Forest Railway also operate seasonal passenger services over a short stretch of the Lydney-Parkend line, which (apart from a section of the old Chepstow-Monmouth branch to Tidenham Quarry) is now the only other surviving part of the once numerous Forest of Dean and Wye Valley lines. At Coleford a small railway museum, commemorating these lines, has been established in the ex-Great Western goods shed.

The City of Birmingham has its own steam centre at Tyseley where a number of ex-Great Western locomotives are kept on the site of the old steam depot. Incidentally the adjacent diesel depot is now the main servicing and repair depot for Centro and Regional Railways Class 150, 153 and 156 units.

The Border regions which were once criss-crossed by a number of branch lines are today served by the Newport, Shrewsbury and Chester line, and in the south by the Chepstow-Gloucester line. This latter line is also used as a diversionary route to and from South Wales in the event of problems with the Severn Tunnel. Apart from the passenger traffic both are still important cross-country freight routes.

Since the closure in 1975 of the ex-Midland Railway station at Gloucester Eastgate all services to and from Gloucester use the ex-Great Western 'Central' station. At Cheltenham the opposite has occurred, for since the closure of the ex-Great Western stations at Malvern Road and St James in 1966, all services now use the ex-Midland station at Lansdown. Main line services between Cheltenham, Gloucester and Paddington, which are today operated by InterCity HSTs, still run over the 'Golden Valley' route via Stroud, Kemble and Swindon. Local services between Gloucester and Swindon are operated by Regional Railways using Class 150 and 158 units. Another line that has survived against all odds is the Cotswold line between Oxford and Worcester. The line, which is also operated by Regional Railways, was singled during the 1970s. Many of the stations however are still open, and although the line is no longer used for through freight traffic, it continues to provide an important passenger link between the Cathedral cities of Oxford, Worcester and Hereford.

The whole of the West Midland and Border areas still provides a considerable amount of freight traffic with all classes of railfreight, but particularly coal, oil and freightliner traffic, passing through on a daily basis. As with the rest of the ex-Great Western system. freight services are now operated using Classes 37, 47, 56 and 60.

Fenny Compton
An ex-WD 'Austerity' class 2-8-0 No 90052 pauses at Fenny Compton on Sunday 24 September 1961 whilst *en route* from Stratford-on-Avon to Woodford Halse via the ex-Stratford-on-Avon & Midland Junction route. The remains of the S&MJR station, Fenny Compton West, which closed on 7 April 1952, can be seen on the left. On the right is the Great Western main line to Birmingham and the down platform of the GW station is just behind the loco.

On 15 November 1993 Class 166 Turbo No 166212 runs through with the Thames Line service to Stratford-on-Avon. The signalbox which was opened on 7 March 1960 is still very much in use. The old S&MJR route is now open only as far as the military base at Kineton (currently used for secure storage of surplus coaching stock).
M. Mitchell/Author

Leamington
Seventy years separate these three shots of Leamington. The first was taken in 1923 and shows De Glehn 4-4-2 No 103 *President* at the up platform with a cross-country service to the south coast. Notice the footbridge in the background, the cattle dock in the left foreground and the original station canopy. The station was rebuilt in 1938. A new subway replaced the old footbridge. The new canopy on the up-side can be seen in this shot of 'Hall' class 4-6-0 No 5926 *Grotrian Hall* after arrival with the 12.50pm service from Birmingham on 31 May 1960. On the right and behind the running-in board part of the ex-LNWR station at Leamington Spa (Avenue) can just be seen.

The same scene on 16 November 1993 shows Class 47 No 47820 on the 2.44pm service to Reading. Avenue station closed on 18 January 1965, but interestingly InterCity services to Birmingham now use the ex-LNWR route between Leamington and Coventry.
Author's Collection/ M. Mensing/Author

Warwick

The 7.45pm service from Leamington Spa to Stratford-on-Avon hauled by '5100' class 2-6-2T No 4118 stands at Warwick on 8 May 1958. In the bay stands fellow class member No 4128 on Hatton banking duties.

   The original station building still stands but the bay is now filled in; its outline can still be seen. On 16 November 1993 a Class 165 Turbo No 165025 arrives with the 8.31am service from Leamington to Snow Hill. *M. Mensing/Author*

Hatton

Hatton station is situated at the top of Hatton Bank. The station is pictured here in April 1957 as 2-6-2T No 5185 arrives with a service from Leamington to Birmingham Moor Street. Hatton South box (seen just behind the loco) was closed on 1 September 1969.

On 16 November 1993 Class 150 Sprinter No 150129 arrives with a Snow Hill-Leamington stopping service. Today Hatton is unstaffed and passenger facilities are certainly basic.
Real Photos/Author

Hatton South junction

'Castle' class 4-6-0 No 5056 *Earl of Powis* with an up parcels from the Birmingham area passes Hatton South junction in July 1964.

On 16 November 1993 Class 153 unit No 153383 runs on to the Stratford branch with the 9am service from Leamington to Stratford-on-Avon. At one time there was a triangular junction here but in recent years the North junction connection has been removed.
Real Photos/Author

Claverdon

A service from Stratford to Leamington hauled by 'Grange' class No 6851 *Hurst Grange* pulls into Claverdon in April 1957. The line was singled in November 1968 and now only the up platform remains. On 27 November 1993 I waited for over an hour in sub-zero conditions only to be told by a local taxi driver that the services had been cancelled, hence the lack of train!
Real Photos/Author

Bearley

A general view of Bearley station in the 1920s. This was the junction station for the branch to Great Alne and Alcester (closed to passengers on 25 September 1939). The signalbox controlled the small goods yard and the east junction.

Both platforms were shortened on 10 December 1966, and the signalbox was closed on 17 December 1967. On 15 November 1993 what remains at Bearley can be seen as 'Heritage' set No 117210 arrives with the 2.4pm service to Stratford-on-Avon; there were no passengers!
Ian Allan Library/Author

Stratford-on-Avon

A view of Stratford-on-Avon station taken from the adjacent roadbridge in 1947. At this time the line continued south and through to Cheltenham. The station seen here was built in 1911, replacing an earlier station which had stood on the same site.

Local services were withdrawn between Stratford and Cheltenham on 7 March 1960, but the line remained open as a through route for goods and diversions until 15 March 1976.

Today Stratford is the terminus for North Warwickshire line services to Birmingham and also services to Leamington and Paddington via Oxford. The station shows little change as Sprinter No 150009 waits at platform 1 on 15 November 1993 with the 1.20pm service to Shirley. Platforms 2 and 3 now appear to be used only at peak times.
R. C. Riley/Author

Bearley East junction

The diverted 9.40am Paddington-Wolverhampton service hauled by 'Castle' No 5044 *Earl of Dunraven* traverses the loop at Bearley East junction on 24 May 1959. At this time the line had seen little use other than for diversions since the complete closure of the Alcester Branch in 1951. In the background is Bearley station.

The course of the loop is still discernible (just) in this picture taken on 15 November 1993. In the background is the single track line to Bearley West junction.
T. E. Williams/Author

Henley-in-Arden

Henley-in-Arden was originally served by a short branch from the GW main line at Rowington. The original terminus station at Henley was closed to passengers on 1 July 1908 (it remained open for goods until 5 November 1962). For the opening of the North Warwickshire line on 1 December 1907 a new station was constructed at Henley-in-Arden. It is seen here in March 1957 as 2-6-2T No 3101 arrives with a service from Moor Street.

Apart from the removal of the buildings on the island platform, little has changed at Sprinter No 150013 arrives with the 10.22am service from Birmingham Snow Hill to Stratford on 27 November 1993.
Real Photos/Author

Earlswood Lakes

Earlswood Lakes pictured here in April 1957 as 2-6-2T No 4170 arrives with a service from Stratford-on-Avon to Birmingham Moor Street. The suffix Lakes was dropped from 6 May 1974. On 27 November 1993 passengers board Sprinter No 150001 on the 11.46am service from Stratford to Snow Hill. Rationalisation has seen all station buildings removed and passengers are now required to cross the line via the adjacent road bridge.
Real Photos/Author

Shirley

Shirley has always been one of the busier stations on the North Warwickshire line. On 29 August 1959 an ex-Great Western '4300' class 2-6-0 No 5332 slowly moves through the station with a down freight.

Shirley today forms part of the southern suburbs of Birmingham and is served by a half hourly Sprinter service to and from Snow Hill. On 27 November 1993 Sprinter No 150124 arrives with a service from Snow Hill. The signalbox here is still open and can just be seen beyond the footbridge. The old Great Western signal has however been replaced by an upper quadrant type.
M. Mensing/Author

Knowle & Dorridge

Back on the main line as the 8.5am service from Birkenhead to Paddington passes Knowle & Dorridge on 13 March 1955 hauled by 'King' class 4-6-0 No 6014 *King Henry VIII*. The signalbox was closed on 1 September 1969 when control passed to the new power box at Saltley. Looking down from the same overbridge on 16 November 1993 Turbo Class 165 No 165032 speeds through with a service from Snow Hill to Marylebone. Standing in the down relief platform is a Class 150 Sprinter on a stopping service to Snow Hill.
M. Mensing/Author

Olton

The 5.10pm service from Birmingham Snow Hill to Knowle & Dorridge leaves platform 3 at Olton station on 26 September 1961 hauled by 2-6-2T No 6101. As with other stations on the line, rationalisation in 1968 saw platforms 3 and 4 close. Permission to cross the line on to the old platform (left) to recreate the shot was not forthcoming so the 'Now' picture was taken from platform 2, where on 16 November 1993 a Class 150 Sprinter speeds through *en route* to Dorridge.
M. Mensing/Author

Solihull

The 3.10pm service from Paddington to Wolverhampton hauled by 'King' No 6003 *King George IV* accelerates away from Solihull on 30 May 1960. The goods yard on the left was closed in stages between June 1962 and February 1965. Both up and down relief lines were removed in July 1968 and on a misty 27 November 1993 the scene has changed completely as Sprinter No 150014 approaches the station with a service to Leamington.
M. Mensing/Author

Acocks Green & South Yardley

Ex-Great Western 2-6-2T No 5163 stands at platform 3 at Acocks Green & South Yardley in March 1967 with a service from Moor Street to Leamington. Again this was another station that was enlarged by the Great Western in 1933.

On 16 November 1993 Sprinter 150202 arrives at Acocks Green (the South Yardley was dropped in the 1970s) with a Snow Hill-Leamington service. The relief lines were taken out of use between Tyseley and Solihull in July 1968. Today the site of platforms 3 and 4 form the station car park. *Real Photos/Author*

Tyseley South box
Looking south from the roadbridge BR Class 9F 2-10-0 No 92208 runs past Tyseley South box. This controlled the North Warwickshire line junction, it was closed on 1 September 1969. On a rather misty 27 November 1993 Sprinter Class 150 No 150124 departs with a service to Stratford-on-Avon. Signalling in the area is now controlled from the power box at Saltley. Notice also that the church on the right of the first picture has lost its tower.
P. J. Sharpe/Author

Tyseley
The 9.30am service from Bournemouth West to Birkenhead runs through Tyseley on 29 August 1959 hauled by a pair of 'Hall' class 4-6-0s Nos 4990 *Clifton Hall* and 4902 *Aldenham Hall*.

Because of its close proximity to the steam centre the station at Tyseley has been tastefully restored back to Great Western condition. This can be seen as a 'Heritage' Class 117 No 117213 runs through on a semi-fast service to Leamington.
M. Mensing/Author

Small Heath & Sparkbrook
The 4.50pm service from Birmingham Snow Hill to Lapworth hauled by '6100' class 2-6-2T No 6166 arrives at Small Heath & Sparkbrook on 30 March 1957. A station was first opened here in 1863 but the station pictured here was constructed by the Great Western during the quadrupling of the lines in 1933.

Platforms 1 and 2 are currently closed and with access denied my 'now' photograph was taken from platform 3 where Class 150 No 150126 arrives with a semi-fast service to Dorridge. *M. Mensing/Author*

Birmingham Moor Street

The main station for Great Western suburban services south of Birmingham was at Moor Street. The decision to reopen Snow Hill also saw the construction of a new station at Moor Street. The new station is situated just south of Snow Hill tunnel on the course of the old main line. The old station at Moor Street was closed on the same day as the new station was opened, 2 October 1987.

The original formation can be seen in this picture of an up parcels train hauled by 'Grange' class 4-6-0 No 6853 *Morehampton Grange* leaving Snow Hill tunnel on 27 February 1960. The tunnel was closed on 4 March 1968.

On 16 November 1993 a pair of Sprinter units Nos 150014 and 150009 call at the new Moor Street *en route* to Snow Hill and Dorridge respectively. The third picture shows the now derelict ex-Great Western station.
M. Mensing/Author

Birmingham Snow Hill
The fine frontage and entrance to Snow Hill station in Colmore Row. It was built by the Great Western as a hotel in 1863 but due to lack of patronage it was closed in 1909 and subsequently converted into offices. The partial closure of Snow Hill in 1968 saw the building fall out of use and in 1969 it was demolished. The entrance to Snow Hill today is still in Colmore Row but via the twin canopies in the centre of the Sun Alliance building.
D. Bickley/Author

Birmingham Snow Hill
Empty stock from the 8.50am service from Margate to Birmingham is hauled through Birmingham Snow Hill on 16 August 1958 by ex-Great Western '4300' class 2-6-0 No 6361. At the time of writing the lines terminate here, but work is in progress to re-lay the line northwards and connect with the Kidderminster line at Smethwick West.
M. Mensing/Author

Birmingham Snow Hill

Birmingham Snow Hill looking south, pictured here from the North signalbox in the 1920s. The first station at Snow Hill opened on 1 October 1852 but with the increase in traffic was soon enlarged. The station pictured here was constructed in 1906. The run-down of services saw the station reduced to an unstaffed halt in 1968, being finally closed on 6 March 1972. It was soon demolished, the site being used for a number of years as a car park.

The revival of railways in the Birmingham area under the banner of the West Midlands PTE saw a new station opened at Snow Hill on 2 October 1987. The platforms, as can be seen in this view taken on 16 November 1993, are situated under a multi-storey car park.
GW Trust/Author

Wolverhampton Low Level

This view of Wolverhampton Low Level station was taken on 16 June 1957. Standing in the up main platform is ex-Great Western 4-4-0 No 3440 *City of Truro* on a Stephenson Locomotive Society special to Swindon Works. In the bay platform is 2-6-2T No 5106 on a service to Kidderminster and Worcester.

Wolverhampton Low Level was closed on 6 March 1972 and looks in remarkable condition in this shot taken on 16 November 1993. The station building is being restored but I understand the rest of the site is being developed into some kind of sports stadium.
G. F. Bannister/Author

Wellington

Wellington was at one time a major junction for Great Western services to Nantwich, Buildwas Junction, Wolverhampton and Shrewsbury and also for LNWR services to Stafford and Coalport. Sadly today only the Wolverhampton-Shrewsbury line remains. In this September 1964 picture a Standard Class 5, No 73097, on a Shrewsbury-Stafford stopping service is overtaken by 'Manor' class 4-6-0 No 7806 *Cockington Manor* on the up 'Cambrian Coast Express'. Just behind the Class 5 is the coaling plant for the ex-Great Western steam depot. This was closed on 10 August 1964.

In the ensuing years the various bay platforms have been closed and the down platform canopy has been shortened. Since the construction of Telford New Town the station is now designated Wellington Telford West. On 15 September 1993 Class 150 Sprinter No 150014 arrives with the 3.9pm service from Chester to Birmingham New Street. *R. Cowlishaw/Author*

Shrewsbury

The up 'Cambrian Coast Express' hauled by 'Manor' class 4-6-0 No 7828 *Odney Manor* waits at Shrewsbury on 11 September 1963. Shrewsbury was and still is an important junction and interchange point for services to Chester, Crewe, Wolverhampton, Aberystwyth and Pwllheli. The station originally had an overall roof but this was removed many years ago. To say the loading of Cambrian line services has changed would be an understatement, which is illustrated in this picture of single car Class 153 No 153371 standing at platform 4 with the 1.53pm (Sundays-only) service to Pwllheli. *D. Tuck/Author*

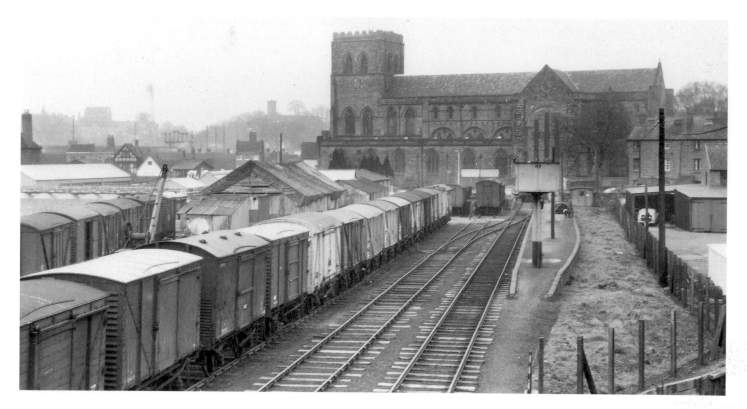

Shrewsbury Abbey

The ex-Shropshire & Montgomery station at Shrewsbury Abbey. The station was closed to passengers on 6 November 1933 but in this March 1960 shot the platform is still *in situ* on the right. The yard continued to be used for goods until 7 October 1968 and an oil depot survived until the late 1980s on the site. The abbey is the obvious reference point in this picture taken on 15 September 1993 . The foreground area now forms a car park for a large supermarket (behind photographer).
R. C. Riley/Author

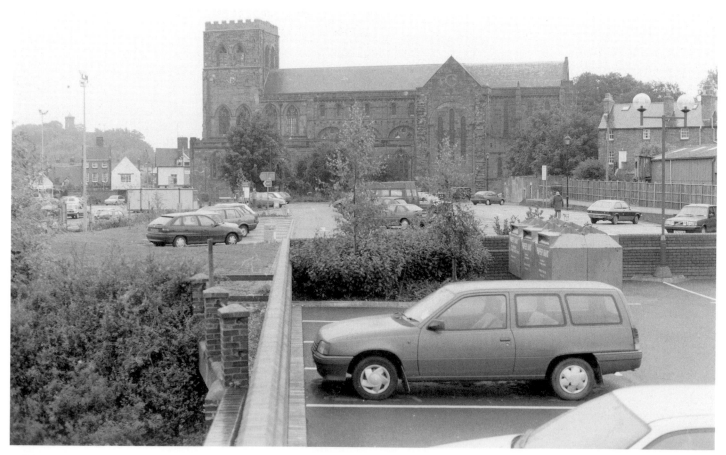

Stourbridge Town

Stourbridge Town station is situated on a short branch that leaves the Birmingham-Worcester line at Stourbridge Junction. The station is pictured here on the evening of 8 September 1956 as 0-4-2T No 1458 prepares to depart with the 9.22pm service to Stourbridge Junction.

The line originally continued for another half-mile or so to serve a small goods yard but this section was closed in 1965. Today part of the old platform has been adapted for modern needs with basic facilities. On 15 November 1993 Class 153 unit No 153381 waits to leave with the 10.19am service to Stourbridge Junction.
M. A. Walker /Author

Kidderminster

Kidderminster is situated on the former Great Western line from Worcester to Birmingham. It was also the junction station for the Severn Valley line to Shrewsbury. This line was closed to passengers on 7 September 1963, but was subsequently taken over by the Severn Valley Railway who now operate passenger services from their new station at Kidderminster through to Bridgnorth. The ex-Great Western station at Kidderminster is pictured here on 2 August 1961. The platform was extended under the road bridge in the early 1920s. The station signalbox was closed on 15 July 1973. The main station buildings were removed in the 1960s and replaced by a simple brick structure. Notice also how the down platform has been shortened.
GW Trust/Barrie Fenton

Kidderminster

On a misty autumn morning in 1958 an ex-Great Western 0-6-0PT No 4613 departs from the up bay at Kidderminster with the Kidderminster portion of the 'Cathedrals Express'.

On 15 November 1993 Sprinter No 150013 passes the same spot with the 12.15pm service to Hereford. The large goods shed on the left is now used as a carriage works by the Severn Valley Railway.
GW Trust/Author

Bewdley

Bewdley was once an important junction station on the Severn Valley line with services to Shrewsbury, Kidderminster, Stourport and Tenbury Wells. A view from the footbridge at Bewdley on 10 August 1957, shows an ex-GW diesel railcar on a Kidderminster service.

Apart from the addition of some enamel advertising signs and some additional stock, the station remains almost unchanged.
Norman Simmons/Author

Arley

Ex-Great Western diesel railcar No W32 in BR green livery pauses at Arley in the early 1960s with a service to Kidderminster.

The station at Arley has now been restored back to its former glory and has since won many awards. Only the modern coach in the siding betrays the fact that this shot was taken on 15 November 1993 and not in the 1930s.
J. Spencer-Gilks/Author

Bridgnorth

Ex-LMS 2-6-2T No 41209 with the 7.27pm service to Shrewsbury waits at Bridgnorth on 6 September 1963, the penultimate day of passenger services between Bewdley and Shrewsbury. The Ivatt 2-6-2Ts were regular performers during the last years of operation over the line. This section of the branch was taken over by the Severn Valley Railway on 23 May 1970 and since that date has been the operating centre of the line. Looking from the same spot on 15 November 1993 the scene is relatively unchanged except some preserved ex-BR Mk 1 stock now occupies the platform.
Hugh Ballantyne/Author

Kemble junction

The line from Swindon junction to Kemble was opened by the Great Western Union Railway on 31 May 1841, and from Kemble to Gloucester on 12 May 1845. Looking south from the footbridge at Kemble junction in May 1932 a Great Western '4300' class 2-6-0 waits with a Gloucester-Paddington service. Standing in the Cirencester bay on the left is a '517' class 0-4-2T. The branch from Kemble to Cirencester Town was opened on 31 May 1841; it was closed to passengers on 6 April 1964. Looking down from the footbridge on 18 January 1994 a Class 150 Sprinter unit No 150253 departs with a service to Swindon. Notice the track still *in situ* in the bay platform.
GW Trust/Peter Heath

Cirencester Town
As already mentioned Cirencester Town was the terminus of a 4½-mile branch that ran from Kemble junction. The station which was opened on 31 May 1841 is said to have been designed by Brunel but is probably the work of his assistant Brereton. The station is pictured here in the 1950s. Standing at the single platform is an ex-Great Western '5700' class 0-6-0PT No 3739 on a service to Kemble. Steam traction was withdrawn in 1960 and replaced by single car railbuses; unfortunately these were not entirely successful and passenger traffic was withdrawn on 6 April 1964. The unusual station building is now listed, the platform area and yard being used as a car and bus park.
D. Lawrence/Author

Brimscombe
In Great Western days a number of small stations and halts were constructed to serve the communities along the line. Brimscombe was at the start of the climb up to Sapperton. A small single road engine shed was situated adjacent to the station to house the banking engines. For many years local services were in the hands of '517' class and '4800' class 0-4-2Ts. On 25 September 1960 '4800' class 0-4-2T No 1409 and autocoach W238 runs into Brimscombe with the 2.05pm 'Chalford Flyer' service from Gloucester to Chalford. Brimscombe was closed to passengers on 2 November 1964 and was soon removed. The only obvious reference point is the large evergreen tree seen behind Sprinter No 150253 as it passes the site of the old station with the 1.20pm service from Gloucester to Swindon on 28 October 1993.
Hugh Ballantyne/Peter Heath

Frampton Mansell

From Kemble the line to Gloucester ran via Sapperton and down through the 'Golden Valley'. A particularly scenic section is at Frampton Mansell where the line crosses part of the valley on a nine arch viaduct. It is seen here on 8 June 1963 as '7200' class 2-8-2T No 7209 crosses with an up goods. The viaduct now has a rather weathered look as Sprinter No 150283 drifts by with the 11.59am service from Gloucester to Swindon on 28 October 1993.
Dr Geoff Smith/Peter Heath

Stonehouse (Burdett Road)
The 4.40pm service from Gloucester to Chalford hauled by '5700' class 0-6-0PT No 8743 pauses at Stonehouse (Burdett Road) on 2 June 1962.

Now reduced to an unstaffed halt, the station is pictured here in August 1993 as Sprinter No 150221 leaves with a service from Swindon to Cheltenham.
L. Sandler/Author

Stroud

This interesting picture shows Great Western steam railmotor No 5 on a Chalford to Gloucester service at Stroud station, and possibly soon after the service was inaugurated in October 1903. The service, which was eventually worked using '4800' class 0-4-2Ts, was withdrawn from 2 November 1964. The station at Stroud has survived remarkably well and is pictured here on 18 January 1994 as Class 158 No 158837 arrives with a Swindon-Gloucester service. *GW Trust/Peter Heath*

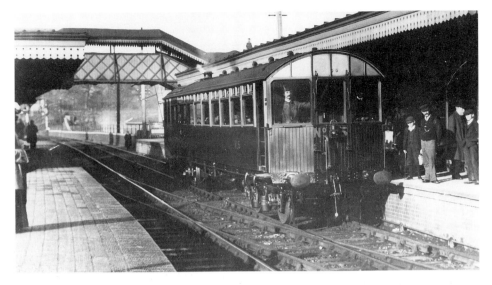

Fosse Cross

The M&SWJ station at Fosse Cross stood on the northern section of the M&SWJR. The station, pictured here in 1959, was situated about one mile down a country lane from the nearest main road (Fosse Way). The M&SWJR once had an engine shed here but this was closed during World War 1. The station closed to passengers on 11 September 1961.

The platform face can still be seen on 26 October 1993, the station building has been re-roofed and is now used as a grain store by the local farmer. *J. D. Edwards/Peter Heath*

183

Kingham

'Castle' class 4-6-0 No 7004 *Eastnor Castle* arrives at Kingham on 11 May 1963 with the 4.5pm service from Hereford to Paddington. Kingham was the junction for the Cheltenham-Banbury branch. The station is still staffed and is now one of the passing points on the Cotswold Line. The remains of the Chipping Norton and Cheltenham bay can be seen on the right as Thames Turbo No 166207 arrives on 22 October 1993 with the 8.47am service from Worcester Foregate Street to Paddington.
B. Ashworth/Peter Heath

Stow-on-the-Wold

A pair of spotters sit on the platform at Stow-on-the-Wold on 1 September 1958 as 2-6-2T No 5514 arrives with the 9.5am service from Cheltenham to Kingham. Stow stood on the Kingham-Cheltenham section of the Banbury & Cheltenham Direct Railway. The station at Stow was closed to passengers on 15 October 1962 but remained open for goods until 7 September 1964. After closure the station was purchased and has since been converted into a private house, seen here on 10 September 1993.
GW Trust/Author

Bourton-on-the-Water

The next station on the line was at Bourton-on-the-Water. This view, looking west, on 15 August 1955 shows the stone building and the second, stone built, platform. The station closed to passengers on 15 October 1962 but remained open for goods traffic until 7 September 1964. For a number of years after closure the site was used for light industrial use but in recent years has been developed for housing. On 26 October 1993 the station building stands rather out of place in the middle of a housing estate. The bridge has gone but one of the pine trees remains.
GW. Trust/Peter Heath

Adlestrop

Adlestrop station was situated on the Cotswold line about three miles north of Kingham. The station was opened as Adlestrop & Stow Road by the Oxford, Worcester & Wolverhampton Railway in 1853. It was renamed Adlestrop by the Great Western Railway in 1862. This 1920s picture shows the station, goods shed and stationmaster's house. The station was closed on 3 January 1966.

Today all trace of the station has gone except for the station master's house, part of which can just be seen on the left behind the trees, and the station nameboard which together with an ex-Great Western seat from the station are housed in a bus shelter at Adlestrop village (over one mile from the old station).
Real Photos/Author

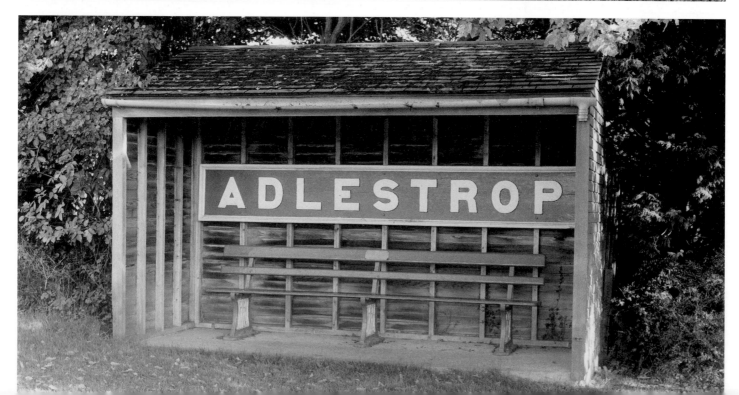

Moreton-in-Marsh

BR Standard 2-6-0 No 78009 stands in the bay platform at Moreton-in-Marsh in 1959 with a brake van special to Shipston-on-Stour. The Shipston branch was actually closed to passenger traffic on 8 July 1929 but had remained open for freight until 2 May 1960.

The old Shipston branch is now just a short siding in this view of Moreton-in-Marsh taken on 10 October 1993. The slightly different angle is due to the fact that the station footbridge has now been shortened. Notice that semaphore signalling is still in use and that the signalbox is still open. *J. D. Edwards/Author*

Worcester Shrub Hill
'Castle' class 4-6-0 No 7027 *Thornbury Castle* pulls the Hereford portion of the up 'Cathedrals Express' into Worcester Shrub Hill in the early 1960s. In the background behind the second coach the roof of the steam depot can just be seen; it closed to steam on 31 December 1965 but continued in use as a diesel stabling point. Semaphore signals are still very much in evidence in this view taken on 10 October 1993. The absence of a train shows the newly refurbished servicing point full of Turbo and Sprinter units.
A. A. Vickers/Author

Great Malvern

The attractive station at Great Malvern was opened by the West Midland Railway on 25 May 1860. The station is seen here in May 1952 as 'Hall' class 4-6-0 No 6992 *Arborfield Hall* arrives with a service to Hereford. In the bay platform is ex-LMS Class 1P 0-4-4T No 58051 on a service to Malvern Wells and Ashchurch. The branch was closed between Great Malvern and Upton-upon-Severn on 1 December 1952 and, today, the old bay has been tastefully transformed into a garden. The station itself is beautifully restored and is a credit to the town.
Real Photos/Author

Ledbury

This super panoramic view shows the station and yard at Ledbury on 15 March 1962. Looking in poor shape is 'Manor' 4-6-0 No 7820 *Dinmore Manor* departing with the 12.05pm service from Hereford to Paddington.

I spent nearly two hours trying to recreate this shot but could not find a suitable gap in the large number of trees that have grown in the ensuing 31 years, so I eventually had to settle for this shot taken from above the tunnel entrance. Not entirely satisfactory but a good enough reason to include the first shot. *A. A. Vickers/Author*

Ledbury

A Birmingham-Cardiff service hauled by 'Hall' class 4-6-0 No 6916 *Misterton Hall* arrives at Ledbury on 5 May 1958.

The station buildings now comprise a single wooden shed, but the signalbox is still *in situ* and in use. The hole in the footbridge is I understand to allow the signalman a view of the down starter signal.
M. Hale/Author

Hereford

A southbound parcels service leaves Hereford on 11 June 1964 behind 'Grange' class 4-6-0 No 6820 *Kingstone Grange*. Hereford was at one time the interchange point for services to Mid Wales, Gloucester, Worcester, Newport and Shrewsbury. Today only the Worcester and Newport-Shrewsbury services remain. I have altered the angle slightly to include the South signalbox, which is still in use, as a Class 60 No 60093 *Jack Stirk*, restarts a Cardiff-bound freight after a crew change on 6 November 1993.

The station itself has seen little change although many of the adjacent sidings have now gone. Since the closure of the steam shed in 1964 locomotives have been stabled in a bay at the north end of the down platform.
D. Cross/Author

Ludlow

'Castle' class 4-6-0 No 7011 *Banbury Castle* rushes through Ludlow on 8 June 1960 with the 8.15am service from Bristol Temple Meads to Crewe. On the right is St Laurence's parish church. The high vantage point of the 1960 picture has now gone so to try and raise the 'now' viewpoint somewhat I stood on a large pile of bricks. The obvious reference points are the church and the goods shed, which closed in 1965 but is now used by a local hauliers. On 14 September 1993 a Class 158 unit No 158828 departs from Ludlow with the 12.8pm service to Shrewsbury. *C. P. Walker /Author*

Woofferton

'4800' class 0-4-2T No 1455 stands at the ex-Shrewsbury & Hereford joint station at Woofferton on 27 July 1957 with a Stephenson Locomotive Club special commemorating the centenary of the Kington branch. Woofferton was the junction for the short branch to Tenbury Wells. Woofferton was closed to passengers together with the branch on 31 July 1961. The main building now survives as a private house and is pictured here on 14 September 1993. *G. F. Bannister/Author*

Gloucester Central

A busy time at Gloucester Central. On the left '4800' class 0-4-2T No 1424 arrives with the 11.40am service from Chalford, in the background a '2251' class 0-6-0 prepares to leave with the 12.25pm service to Hereford and on the right '4300' class 2-6-0 No 6365 stands with the 12.35pm (SO) service to Cheltenham. The adjacent Midland station at Eastgate was closed on 1 December 1975 and since that date all services have used the former Great Western station. The station was rebuilt in May 1968. The work included a considerable extension to platform 1, thus allowing all services to use this platform. On 6 November 1993 an HST arrives with the 6.40am service from Newcastle to Penzance, which reverses here. The old up platform (right) is now used for parcels traffic. *B. Ashworth/Author*

Tramway junction, Gloucester

An ex-Great Western '2884' class 2-8-0 No 3824 passes Tramway junction, Gloucester with a freight for Worcester on 30 January 1964. Behind the locomotive is Tramway Junction signalbox and behind that the ex-Great Western locomotive shed at Horton Road. The shed was closed on 31 December 1965 and the signalbox on 25 May 1968. On 14 December 1993 Class 158 No 158794 departs with the 12.50pm service from Cardiff to Nottingham. The remains of the steam depot, now used as a diesel stabling point, can still be seen. On the left is the Gloucester power box which opened on 25 May 1968. *P. J. Lynch/Author*

Grange Court Junction

Grange Court Junction station was situated on the Gloucester-Chepstow line about seven miles south of Gloucester and was the junction station for the branch to Hereford. On 2 June 1962 '4300' class 2-6-0 No 6330 arrives at the branch platform with the 2.30pm Gloucester-Hereford service. The station was well off the beaten track, the village of Grange Court comprises no more than a few cottages and farms. The station was closed to passengers on 2 November 1964 with the closure of the Hereford branch.

All trace of the station has gone except for the small brick building on the right and the white building seen in both pictures which I believe was the station master's house. On a murky 6 November 1993 Class 158 No 158828 runs past with the 9am service from Cardiff to Nottingham. The line on the left is now used as a goods loop. *J. Spencer-Gilks/Author*

Holme Lacy

One of the intermediate stations on the Gloucester-Hereford branch was at Holme Lacy. On 4 July 1963 the station looks pretty run-down as '4300' class 2-6-0 No 6304 departs with the 1.40pm Hereford-Gloucester service. The station was closed on 2 November 1964. Today the site is almost completely overgrown although part of the platform face can just be seen on the lower right. *A. A. Vickers/Author*

Lydney Junction

Ex-Great Western '4300' class 2-6-0 No 5398 runs through Lydney Junction station with an up freight in the 1950s. At this time Lydney was the junction for passenger services to Sharpness and Lydney Town but these ceased on 26 October 1960. Today part of the old Dean Forest line, from Lydney to Norchard, is operated by the Dean Forest Railway Preservation Society. The signalbox which controlled the adjacent level crossing was reduced to a ground frame in 1969. The station, pictured here in September 1993, is now unstaffed. Today the signalling in the area is controlled by the power box at Newport. *R. E. Toop/Cliff Mannion*

Kerne Bridge

A journey by steam train through the beautifully scenic Wye Valley must have been a wonderful occasion; unfortunately today almost all of the lines have gone. Kerne Bridge, which took its name from an adjacent toll bridge, stood alongside the river on the branch from Monmouth to Ross-on-Wye, and as can be seen even had its own camping coach. On 10 October 1952 '4800' class 0-4-2T No 1455 restarts the 3pm service from Ross to Monmouth. Kerne Bridge was closed to passengers on 5 January 1959.

The large amount of undergrowth has made repeating the first shot almost impossible but the wider angle shows the station building, now in use as an information centre. Notice also the station fencing still *in situ*.
N. Ewart Mitchell/Author

Symonds Yat

Symonds Yat station was also situated adjacent to the river in a very scenic area. The station is seen here on 6 May 1958 as '4800' class 0-4-2T No 1445 leaves with the 11.18am service from Ross-on-Wye to Monmouth. The platform on the right was taken out of use on 1 March 1953. The train is about to enter the 433yd Symonds Yat Tunnel. Standing in the remains of the station loop is an ex-Great Western camping coach. The station was closed together with the line on 5 January 1959.

The station site now forms a car park for the nearby Royal Hotel. I stood on what was the old trackbed to take this picture; behind the hedge both platforms are still *in situ* but the trackbed has now been filled in.
J. Spencer-Gilks/Author

Section 5
Wales

Dyfed, Powys, Gwent, Gwynedd, Clwyd, West, Mid, and South Glamorgan

A selection of GWR publicity posters from the GW Trust's collection.

There was a time when there were probably more lines per square mile in South Wales than any other area of the country. Prior to the Grouping in 1923 (and including the Great Western) services were being operated by no less than 17 different railway companies.

Today this vast railway system that once served every valley has been reduced to just a few lines. It seems that over the years the Principality has had rather more than its fair share of closures. In the south the main centres of Newport, Cardiff and Swansea are well catered for by the InterCity HST services which generally provide an hourly interval service to London. These also serve the three remaining main line stations at Bridgend, Neath and Port Talbot Parkway. Services to Carmarthen and the three remaining branches west of

Swansea are now operated by Regional Railways using Class 150, 155 and 158 units. The branch to Fishguard now only has two services each day which connect with the Rosslare ferry. One of these, the 1.50am is a through HST service to Paddington. Both the Pembroke Dock and Milford Haven branches are served by a two hourly interval service from Swansea; the service usually splits at Whitland. As with the Fishguard line, Milford Haven still retains one direct HST service to and from Paddington each day. The Milford branch is the busiest of the three, as it is traversed by block oil trains running to and from the oil terminals at Milford Haven and Neyland.

Just to the north of Carmarthen a section of the old Aberystwyth branch between Bronwydd Arms and Llwyfan Cerrig has been reopened by the Gwili

Railway Society. The line was originally closed to passengers on 22 February 1965.

One line that seems to have survived against all odds is the ex-London & North Western Railway's Central Wales line from Llandeilo to Craven Arms and Shrewsbury. Services over this route originally ran from Swansea Victoria via Pontardulais junction but since the closure of Swansea Victoria on 15 June 1964 services have departed from Swansea High Street and run via Llanelli. There are currently just four through services a day in each direction. In recent years the Mid Glamorgan County Council has invested a considerable amount of money in the Valley Lines. The Rhymney, Merthyr and Treherbert branches have benefited with the opening of several new stations *en route*. The Aberdare branch, closed to passengers on 15 June 1964,

was reopened for passenger traffic on 3 October 1988 and from 17 May 1993 services were restored to Maesteg (originally closed to passengers on 15 July 1970). Many of the Valley services now run right through to either Barry Island or Penarth.

There is still a considerable amount of freight in the area comprising mainly coal, steel and oil, with yards at Newport, Cardiff and Margam, although the diminishing freight traffic has resulted in the closure of both Severn Tunnel junction and Radyr yards. A number of the old passenger branches are still open for coal and steel traffic. The bulk of these services are operated using Class 37, 47, 56 and 60 diesels. These together with the Valley units and some HST sets are serviced and maintained at the large servicing depot at Cardiff Canton. A smaller servicing depot is still in operation at Swansea Landore but I understand that this is under threat of closure.

North Wales is now famous for its many preserved narrow gauge lines, but the only ex-Great Western standard gauge line still open is the old Cambrian line from Shrewsbury to Aberystwyth and Pwllheli and a short portion of the Blaenau to Bala branch between Blaenau and Trawsfynydd power station (for freight only). A section of the trackbed of the Bala junction-Barmouth line (closed 18 January 1965) has been relaid as a narrow gauge tourist line and has operated since 14 August 1972 as the Bala Lake Railway. The narrow gauge ex-Cambrian Vale of Rheidol line which for a number of years was BR's only steam railway has in recent times been sold to the Brecon Mountain Railway who now operate it. Since September 1963 the ex-Great Western lines in North and Central Wales have been under the control of the Midland Region. It is interesting to reflect that even after the change of control, Swindon-built steam locomotives continued to be used on Cambrian services up until December 1966 when steam traction was withdrawn from the line.

Services over the ex-Cam-brian line are now operated using Class 150 and 155 Sprinter units with services to Pwllheli and Aberystwyth splitting at Machynlleth. To cut costs the line is radio signalled from the Machynlleth Centre. Since the introduction of Sprinter units the small diesel depot at Machynlleth has closed.

It is certainly a salutary exercise to compare a 1950s railway map of Wales with that of today.

Chepstow
'Castle' class 4-6-0 No 4078 *Pembroke Castle* makes a fine sight as it restarts the 7.30am service from Swansea to Cheltenham from Chepstow on 15 April 1952. The gas lamps have gone but part of the original entrance building survives as Sprinter No 150219 departs with the 1.20pm service to Cardiff on 26 September 1993.
N. Ewart Mitchell/Briane Davies

Severn Tunnel Middle Box

The 2.5pm service from Cardiff to Bristol Temple Meads, hauled by Swindon-built Standard Class 4 No 75008, runs past Severn Tunnel Middle box on its approach to the station at Severn Tunnel junction on 21 May 1958. Also in shot are three '4100' class 2-6-2Ts and a '2800' class 2-8-0. The signalbox was closed on 30 November 1968.

The extensive yard (there were at one time over 60 sidings here) has now been closed and lifted. The diesel depot which opened in 1965 was closed in 1989. Looking from the same spot on 26 September 1993 Class 158 No 158829, departs with the 11.20am service from Portsmouth Harbour to Cardiff. A wider angle shows the wasteland once covered by sidings.
S. Rickard/Briane Davies

Pontypool Road

The present station at Pontypool Road was opened on 1 March 1909 and originally comprised a single island platform with a central bay at each end. The station and sidings are pictured here on 11 June 1962 as '2800' class 2-8-0 No 2806 runs through with a Newport-bound freight. Between 1960 and 1967 many of the sidings, including both bays were removed. As can be seen part of the trackbed was used for the construction of the Pontypool bypass which was opened on 14 June 1982.

During November 1993 the remaining station buildings at Pontypool were removed. The rather spartan station is seen here on 14 December 1993 as Class 158 unit No 158832 arrives with the 9.40am service from Cardiff to Manchester. At the up platform is fellow unit No 158838 with the 8.33am service from Manchester to Cardiff.
N. Ewart Mitchell/Author

Monmouth Troy

Monmouth Troy was a major junction for Wye Valley lines to Ross and Chepstow. The junction is seen here in December 1953. On the left an ex-Great Western '5700' class 0-6-0 shunts the small yard. In the centre and standing on the Ross-on-Wye branch, which diverges away to the left, is the Ross service comprising a '4800' class 0-4-2T and auto coach. Diverging away to the right is the branch to Chepstow. Monmouth Troy was closed to passenger traffic on 5 January 1959. However, the line from Monmouth to Tintern Quarry remained open for stone traffic until 6 January 1964.

After closure the station site was used for industrial purposes but this has now been abandoned. The old station building which had stood derelict for a number of years has in recent years been dismantled and removed to the Gloucestershire & Warwickshire Railway where it has been re-erected at Winchcombe. The two river bridges are still *in situ* but on 6 November 1993 the site was empty and becoming increasingly overgrown. *Real Photos/Author*

Newport High Street
A pair of young spotters eagerly take the number of '5700' class 0-6-0PT No 3712 as it arrives at Newport High Street with the 10.10am service from Blaenavon. Waiting to depart from platform 6 with the 11.5am service to Brecon is '2251' class 0-6-0 No 2287. Today platform 6 has been renumbered platform 3 and is now used by up services. On 17 August 1993 a Paddington bound HST prepares to depart. The branch platform on the left was closed around 1966.
R. E. Toop/Author

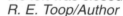

Newport High Street
A view of the down platform at Newport High Street in 1922 and before the station was reconstructed and resignalled. The rebuilding work was completed during 1930, the middle signalbox seen here being closed on 24 June 1928. The station entrance was again modernised in 1973. The station is pictured on 18 August 1993 as an HST arrives with a service from Paddington to Swansea. For a number of years now all services have used the main island platform, the old down platform (right) now being used for parcels traffic. *LGRP/Author*

Crumlin Low Level

Crumlin Low Level station stood on the Western Valleys line from Newport to Aberbeeg. The valley was crossed at this point by the high level Vale of Neath line. The station is pictured here on 6 June 1962 and just a few months after closure (30 April 1962). On the high level Crumlin Viaduct a '6400' class 0-6-0PT crosses with a service from Pontypool Road to Aberdare. A slightly different scene on 26 September 1993: the high level line was closed on 15 June 1964, and the viaduct was demolished soon afterwards. Today the low level line is open as far as the Ebbw Vale steelworks. *GW Trust/Briane Davies*

Aberbeeg
This wonderful view of Aberbeeg was taken in the 1950s and shows both the station and signalbox. The station was situated on the fork of the Brynmawr (right) and Ebbw Vale (left) branches, and was closed to passengers on 30 April 1962. The two large buildings in the centre are the Hanbury Hotel and Webb's Brewery. The scene has certainly changed in this view taken on 16 January 1994. Almost all of the buildings seen in the first picture have been demolished and only the Ebbw Vale branch remains. The signalbox now looks rather isolated.
D. Linekar/Briane Davies

Aberbeeg
This second view, looking towards Newport, was taken on 25 June 1956 and shows the signalbox together with the various carriage sidings. The road from Newport to Aberbeeg which runs along the side of the valley at a much higher level can just be seen on the left. Looking from the same spot on 26 September 1993 the railway has been reduced to the minimum.
P. J. Sharpe/Briane Davies

Pengam junction
'County' class 4-6-0 No 1019 *County of Merioneth* on the 3.50pm Whitland-Kensington milk service stands in the up goods loop at Pengam junction, Cardiff on 19 July 1962. The Roath Dock branch can be seen on the left behind the signalbox.

On Sunday 26 September 1993 a solitary Class 60, No 60033 *Anthony Ashley Cooper*, approaches the junction. The various yards at Pengam have now been closed but the old Roath Dock branch remains open for oil traffic.
R. O. Tuck/Briane

Cardiff General

The 2.25pm Pengam-Llandore freight hauled by 'Grange' class 4-6-0 No 6843 *Poulton Grange* rounds the curve into Cardiff General station on 5 October 1957. The colour-light signals date from the 1934 modernisation programme. On 16 August 1993 Class 158 No 158840 arrives with a service from Portsmouth Harbour. The Central Hotel and the York Hotel (built 1890) can be seen on the left.
R. O. Tuck/Author

Cardiff General

Looking down from the Central Hotel in Coronation week, June 1953 BR Standard 'Britannia' 4-6-2 No 70026 *Polar Star* leaves Cardiff General with the up 'Red Dragon', the 7.30am service from Carmarthen to Paddington. The Great Western opened its first station here in 1850 and since then the station has been greatly expanded. It was extensively rebuilt in 1934 to give the layout that remains today. The station was renamed Cardiff Central on 7 May 1973.

From approximately the same vantage point on 17 August 1993 Class 158 No 158838 arrives with a service from Shrewsbury. Notice how little the station has changed. This part of the Central Hotel is now been converted to student accommodation.
R. C. Riley/Author

Cardiff Queen Street

The ex-Taff Vale station at Cardiff Queen Street is seen here on 29 April 1971 shortly before rebuilding work commenced. The station was enlarged in 1928 to cope with Rhymney Railway services which had been switched from its own station nearby. The present station at Queen Street, seen here on 17 August 1993, was rebuilt during 1973/4. The large building is the Brunel Tower, the Cardiff Division headquarters.
GW Trust/Author

Cardiff Riverside

Cardiff Riverside station pictured here in June 1922. The one-mile long Riverside branch was opened by the Great Western on 14 September 1882. Originally a goods-only line, Barry and Taff Vale passenger services commenced over the branch from 2 April 1894. The station at Cardiff Riverside was rebuilt during 1934 becoming platforms 8 and 9 of the General station. The station was closed to passengers on 16 March 1964 and for a number of years was used as a parcels depot. It is pictured here on 17 August 1993 in a very poor state and sadly by the time this book is in print it will have been demolished to make way for a car park.
P. Rutherford/Author

Barry Town

A Vale of Glamorgan service hauled by ex-Taff Vale 'A' class 0-6-2T No 312 stands at Barry Town on 3 June 1953. Notice the ex-Barry Railway lattice type footbridge. Town was one of four stations at Barry, the others being at Docks, Island and Pier. On 16 August 1993 Sprinter No 150266 arrives with a service from Barry Island to Cardiff Queen Street. The ex-Barry Railway signalbox is still *in situ* and the area is still semaphore signalled. *GW Trust/Author*

Woodham Bros Scrapyard, Barry Dock

For a number of years the No 1 Dock area at Barry was used by Woodham Bros scrap merchants for storing withdrawn steam locomotives prior to cutting up. Although some were reduced to scrap most survived and many of these have since been restored to working order. When I visited the site in 1968 over 200 locomotives were in store. Almost 100 of these can be seen in this picture taken on 9 March 1968. In the foreground are ex-Great Western 'Hall' No 5952 *Cogan Hall*, Standard Class 4 No 76017, and ex-Great Western 'Castle' No 7027 *Thornbury Castle*. Today the site is empty and much of the track has been lifted. *Author*

Barry Island

The ex-Barry Railway station at Barry Island on 20 August 1960. In the foreground at platform 4 is a new DMU on the 1pm service to Merthyr. Standing at platform 3 with some empty stock is a '5600' class 0-6-2T. Arriving with an excursion from the Valleys is another '5600' 0-6-2T No 6687. The station has now been reduced to just one platform, but has a remarkable 20min weekdays interval service to and from Cardiff. On 16 August 1993 a Class 143 arrives with a service from Merthyr.
S. Rickard/Author

Barry Island

Looking in the opposite direction on 2 August 1960 as '5600' class 0-6-2T No 6607 arrives at platform 4 with an excursion. In the background is the small diesel servicing depot. Just to the left of the locomotive is a Barry Railway somersault signal. Looking down from the footbridge on 16 August 1993, the area is a scene of desolation . The diesel servicing point was closed during the 1970s. Just in view in the far background is the Pier Tunnel. Barry Pier station was opened on 27 June 1899, and closed to passengers on 19 October 1973.
S. Rickard/Author

Caerphilly

A '5600' class 0-6-2T No 5640 heads a Bargoed-Cardiff freight through Caerphilly station on 26 April 1960. A short distance from the station stood the ex-Rhymney Railway works. The works were constructed in 1901, taken over by the Great Western in 1923 and closed by the Western Region in 1963.

Since the above picture was taken the station has been reduced in size with the closure of platforms 3 and 4; the area is now used as a bus station. 20 August 1993. *S. Rickard/Author*

Caerphilly
A second view of Caerphilly shows a westbound goods service passing platform 3 hauled by '3400' class 0-6-0PT No 3401. On the left of the picture is the entrance to the locomotive works. Looking down from the footbridge on 20 August 1993 we see Sprinter No 150269 arriving with a service to Aberdare.
S. Rickard/Author

Bargoed
The 3pm (SO) service from Newport to Brecon hauled by '5700' class 0-6-0PT No 9616 leaves Bargoed on 2 May 1959. Diverging away to the right is the line to Rhymney and on the left the line to Pant. The Rhymney line remains open but the line to Pant was closed to passengers on 31 December 1962 and to freight on 23 August 1965. The North signalbox seen in the first picture was closed on 9 November 1970 and replaced by a new box, seen on the right of the second picture on 20 November 1993.
S. Rickard/Briane Davies

Hengoed

At Hengoed the High Level Vale of Neath station crossed the Low Level Rhymney station at right angles. The first picture was taken from the High Level platform and shows the Low Level station on 6 June 1962. Notice the brick 'gents' on the down platform.

With the removal of the high level bridge the same angle is not possible, as on 17 August 1993 Class 143 No 143604 arrives with a service from Rymney to Cardiff. The attractive buildings seen in the first view, including the stationmaster's house (right), have all been removed.
GW Trust/Author

Maesycwmmer

Standing on the opposite side of the Rhymney Valley from Hengoed and on the ex-Brecon & Merthyr's Bassaleg junction-Rhymney line was the small station at Maesycwmmer. As can be seen, at this point the line ran under the high level Vale of Neath line. The station is pictured here on 17 March 1962 as a '4200' class 2-8-0T approaches the station with a down mineral train. The viaduct arch immediately behind the '4200' was built on the skew in order to accommodate the sharp curve of B&M track. The two freights on the high level line, hauled by a '5600' class 0-6-2T and '2800' class 2-8-0 are *en route* to Pontypool Road and Aberdare respectively. The high level Vale of Neath line closed on 15 June 1964 and the ex-Brecon & Merthyr line on 31 June 1962. All remains of the station and line at Maesycwmmer have now gone, with a new road on the old trackbed. The Butcher's Arms pub is still very much in evidence as is the viaduct, which is now a listed structure. *GW Trust/Briane Davies*

New Tredegar

New Tredegar was situated on the old Brecon & Merthyr branch from Rhymney Lower to Bedwas and on the eastern side of the Rhymney valley. The station which opened as New Tredegar & Tir Phil was renamed New Tredegar on 1 July 1924. The line served many mining communities and at New Tredegar the nearby West Elliot Colliery. The station is seen here in the 1950s as a '9400' class 0-6-0PT No 9488 waits to leave with the 4.5pm service to Newport. The station was closed to passenger services on 31 December 1962 and on 20 November 1993 the trackbed is being used as a children's play area: notice that part of the old platform face survives.
R. E. Toop/Briane Davies

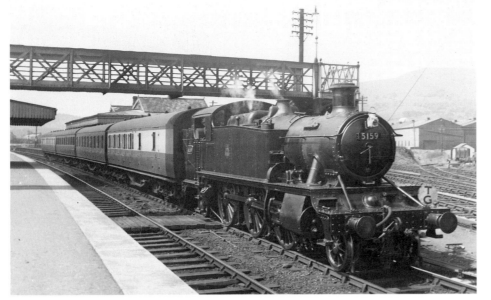

Taffs Well
A Pontypridd-Cardiff service hauled by '5100' class 2-6-2T No 5159 stands at Taffs Well in the 1950s. The high level Penrhos branch crossed the valley here by way of the famous Walnut Tree Viaduct 120ft above, which was closed on 17 June 1963. Taffs Well is still a busy station served by Valley line services. On 18 August 1993 Class 150 Sprinter No 150263 arrives with a Treherbert service. On the left is Taffs Well signalbox, still in operation at the time of writing.
Ian Allan Library/Author

Pontypridd

The busy junction station at Pontypridd seen here on 13 May 1952. A '5600' class 0-6-2T can be seen passing through with a down coal train. The station seen here was built in 1907, the main platform being some 1,500ft long. The station roof and the entrance were rebuilt in 1974. Luckily this is one location where the trees have not obscured the view. On 19 August 1993 Class 37 No 37895 climbs up the valley *en route* to Tower Colliery with an empty MGR service. Only one platform (for services to Cardiff) is now used on the old station. A new platform and footbridge which was opened for services to Merthyr, Aberdare and Treherbert on 25 September 1991 can be seen on the left.
R. C. Riley/Author

Porth

The 1.28pm service from Treherbert to Barry Island hauled by '5600' class 0-6-2T No 5684 approaches Porth on 1 September 1962. Porth was the junction station for the ex-Taff Vale branches to Maerdy (right) and to Treherbert (left). Passenger services were withdrawn to Maerdy on 15 June 1964, but the Treherbert branch is still open and is currently the most successful of the Valley lines. On 16 August 1993 Class 143 No 143617 arrives with the 10.47am service from Treherbert to Penarth. *W. G. Sumner/Author*

Abercynon

A Merthyr-bound freight hauled by '5600' class 0-6-2T No 5691 and banked by '5700' class 0-6-0PT No 9611 runs through Abercynon on 24 September 1964. Abercynon was the junction for the Merthyr and Aberdare branches. Also in view is the four-road steam depot.

Unfortunately since the first picture was taken the hillside has become rather overgrown. The signalbox which is now obscured by the trees is still open but the old steam depot, which after closure in November 1964 was used for light industry, is at the time of writing up for sale. The station has now been reduced to one platform which is used for Merthyr services and renamed Abercynon South. Aberdare line services now stop at Abercynon North (opened 3 October 1988). The single platform is just out of sight behind the trees at the top left of the second picture. *B. J. Ashworth/Author*

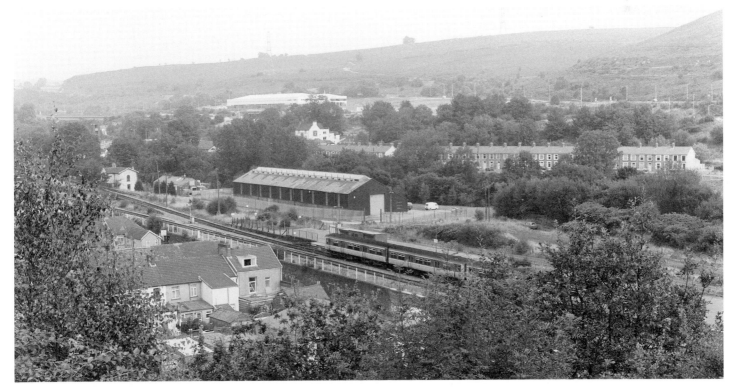

Quaker's Yard Low Level

An ex-Great Western '5700' class 0-6-0PT No 3734 stands at Quaker's Yard Low Level in May 1963. The sidings in the foreground formed a direct connection between the low level and high level lines. The connection and sidings were closed on 15 June 1964 with the closure of the high level line. Since that date the High Level station area and exchange sidings have been used for housing development which makes an exact re-creation impossible. Today only one platform is in use as Sprinter No 150272 arrives with the 11.34am service from Merthyr to Penarth. *A. W. Smith/Author*

Merthyr

The ex-Taff Vale terminus at Merthyr seen here in August 1951. On the left a '5600' class 0-6-0T No 5691 runs around its train. On the right a pair of '6400' class 0-6-0PTs Nos 6434 and 6437 wait on auto services to Dowlais and Pontsticill junction. During 1971 the main station buildings were demolished and replaced by a modern ticket office and platform canopy. Only one platform is now in use as Sprinter No 150272 waits to leave on 16 August 1993 with a service to Penarth. *GW Trust/Author*

Aberdare High Level

The Great Western station at Aberdare High Level was situated on the Vale of Neath line from Pontypool Road to Neath. The branch was closed to passenger traffic on 15 June 1964. The High Level station is pictured here in the 1950s, notice the staggered platforms. The branch remained open for coal traffic as far as Tower Colliery (Hirwaun). Under the Mid Glamorgan County Council's railway development programme the branch was reopened to passenger traffic on 3 October 1988. The £2 million package included new single platform stations at Abercynon North, Penrhiwceiber, Mountain Ash, Fernhill, Cwmbach and Aberdare. Looking north from the new platform on 16 August 1993, the remains of the old High Level station can be seen behind the Sprinter. It is proposed to extend the passenger services through to Hirwaun. *Lens of Sutton/Author*

St Fagans

The 3.45pm service from Paddington to Fishguard Harbour hauled by 'Castle' class 4-6-0 No 7028 *Cadbury Castle* passes St Fagans on 16 July 1955. The station was situated on the Great Western main line just a few miles west of Cardiff. It was reduced to an unstaffed halt on 6 April 1959 and was closed on 10 September 1962. With the footbridge now gone the 'today' picture has been taken from rail level. On 26 September 1993 an HST speeds past the site of the old station with the 3.32pm service from Swansea to Paddington.
J. Hubback/Briane Davies

Llantrisant

Llantrisant station, looking east around the 1920s. The picture was probably taken from the East signalbox and shows in the centre the South Wales main line to Cardiff. The line coming in from the right is the Taff Vale branch from Aberthaw. The station was closed to passengers on 2 November 1964. In 1993 and in connection with the reintroduction of passenger services to Maestag a new station, Pontyclun, was opened on the site of Llantrisant. The new station is pictured here on 20 November 1993. *Lens of Sutton/Briane Davies*

Tondu
A Bridgend-Blaengwynfi service leaves Tondu on 7 July 1962 hauled by '5100' class 2-6-2T No 4121. The line on the right is the Blackmill branch and on the left the Bridgend and Abergwynfi line. Tondu engine shed was situated within the triangle of lines and can just be seen on the right.

The same scene but from a slightly different angle on 20 November 1993 shows the old Tondu Middle signalbox still *in situ*. The line on the right to Blackmill was closed to passengers on 5 May 1958. The Abergwynfi branch remained open for passenger traffic until 5 May 1970; the remains of the branch weres retained as far as Lynfi junction to serve a coal washery plant, and during 1993 as part of the Valley Lines improvements passenger services were reinstated to Maesteg. *S. Pickard/Briane Davies*

Port Talbot General

'Castle' class No 5087 *Tintern Abbey* arrives at Port Talbot General on 9 March 1961 with the 12.5pm service from Milford Haven to Paddington. The station was extensively rebuilt in 1961/2 to give a single island platform which can be seen under construction on the left, and during the 1980s the station was renamed Port Talbot Parkway. The absence of a footbridge has meant that the 'today' shot had to be taken from platform level but the hill in the background together with the island platform is the reference point in this picture taken on 17 August 1993. The branch to Aberavon Town was closed on 3 December 1962 and in the last few years many of the houses on the right have been demolished to make way for a new road.
J. Hodge/Author

Neath General

A down stopping service hauled by 'Hall' class 4-6-0 No 5902 *Howick Hall* pulls into Neath General on 28 August 1959. The station seen here was built in 1877 replacing an earlier structure. It survived almost intact until it was extensively rebuilt during 1977/8 to provide a new entrance and platform buildings. The second illustration shows the current layout at Neath. The centre road was removed in June 1967.
M. Hale/Briane Davies

Swansea High Street

'Castle' class 4-6-0 No 4090 *Dorchester Castle* waits to depart from Swansea High Street on 8 September 1961 with the last up steam-hauled 'South Wales Pullman', the 4.30pm service to Paddington. The station was extensively rebuilt in 1926/7 to provide four main platforms and one bay. The bay was removed in 1973 and, during 1983, to allow for the extension of the station forecourt, the platform lines were shortened by about 100ft.

   Because of current platform reconstruction work I was not able to re-shoot the scene from the same angle. On 17 August 1993 HST 43149 waits with the 12.32pm service to Paddington, whilst leaving platform 4 is Class 158 No 158870 with the 10.34am service from Milford Haven to Portsmouth Harbour. *Hugh Ballantyne/Author*

Llanelly

'Castle' class 4-6-0 No 4081 *Warwick Castle* approaches Llanelly (now Llanelli) with the 11.55am service from Paddington to Milford Haven on 30 August 1960. The signalbox was closed on 10 December 1973 and today the crossing is of the automatic type; Class 153 No 153361 departs with the 1.30pm service from Pembroke Dock to Swansea.
A. Smith/Geoff Wright

Llanelly

Looking west from the same spot on 30 August 1960, as 'Castle' class 4-6-0 No 5067 *St Fagans Castle* departs from Llanelly station with the 3.50pm Whitland-Kensington milk train.

Apart from the removal of the water tower the station has changed little as Class 153 No 153368 departs with the 2.34pm service from Milford Haven to Swansea.
A. Smith/Geoff Wright

Llandilo

Llandilo (now Llandeilo) stands on the ex-GW/LNWR joint route from Llanelli to Craven Arms. A short branch connected Llandilo with the Carmarthen-Aberystwyth line at Abergwili. On 8 June 1960 a '5700' class 0-6-0PT No 9788 arrives at Llandilo with the 6.55pm service from Llandovery. The up platform buildings and footbridge have now been removed but the stone entrance to the down platform remains. On 6 September 1993 both platforms are occupied: on the right Class 153 No 153361 arrives with the 10.20am service from Crewe to Swansea, while on the left No 153302 prepares to leave with the 12.10pm service from Cardiff Central to Shrewsbury. *Hugh Ballantyne/Geoff Wright*

Carmarthen

'7400' class 0-6-0PT No 7439 departs from Carmarthen in the early 1960s, with the 11.35am service to Llandilo. The large building on the left is the ex-Great Western engine shed. This was closed on 13 April 1964. Services north of Carmarthen, to Llandilo and Aberystwyth, were withdrawn on 22 February 1965 .

With the reduction in services, only the old down platform is still in use. The station is seen here on 8 September 1993 as Sprinter No 150282 waits to depart with the 10.31am service to Swansea. Standing at the disused platform with an empty timber train is Class 47 No 47361 *Wilton Endeavour*. *G. T. Robinson/Geoff Wright*

Whitland

The 12.05pm service from Milford Haven to Paddington hauled by '4300' class 2-6-0 No 7318 stands at Whitland in May 1959. This was, and still is, an important interchange point for West Wales services. This is illustrated in this picture taken on 23 September 1993 which shows on the right No 153272 on the 3.14pm service to Pembroke Dock and No 153353 on the 3.16pm service to Milford Haven (the service splits here). On the right is Sprinter No 150272 with the 3.13pm service to Carmarthen and Swansea. The one time steam depot was situated in the yard on the left. *J. F. Aylard/Geoff Wright*

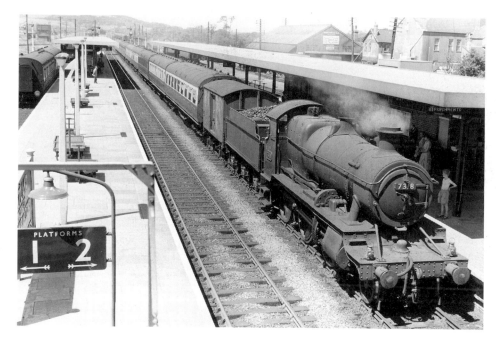

Whitland
This second view of Whitland station was taken on 24 February 1953. Standing at the up platform is an unidentified 'Hall' with the up 'Pembroke Coast Express'. The station was rebuilt in 1958 when many of the old buildings were removed. The rather spartan station is seen here on 23 September 1993 as Class 153 No 153312 departs with the 10.14am service to Pembroke Dock.
GW Trust/Geoff Wright

Cardigan

Cardigan was served by a branch that left the main line west of Whitland. On 31 July 1959 '4500' class 2-6-2T No 4550 prepares to leave with the 5.45pm service to Whitland. The branch was closed on 27 May 1963. The site of the station is now used by a transport company so rather than include a photograph of dozens of stored trailers I have included a picture of the goods shed still intact and seen on the right in the first photograph.
R. O. Tuck/Geoff Wright

Boncath

One of the intermediate stations on the Cardigan branch was at Boncath. The station is seen here on 28 August 1956 as '4500' class 2-6-2T No 4550 arrives with the 11.35am service from Whitland. The station was closed with the branch on 27 May 1963 and lay derelict for a number of years before being sold. In this shot taken on 26 September 1993 the trackbed has been swallowed up in the undergrowth, but the platform face can still be seen under the accumulating rubbish.
G. F. Bannister/Geoff Wright

Narberth

The 1pm service from Pembroke Dock to Paddington, the 'Pembroke Coast Express', leaves Narberth station on 20 July 1963 hauled by 'Manor' class 4-6-0 No 7814 *Fringford Manor*. The locomotive will be replaced at Swansea with a 'Castle'. Narberth was a crossing point on the single line Whitland-Pembroke Dock branch. The down platform has now gone but the old goods shed remains and can be seen behind Sprinter No 150270 as it leaves Narberth with the 9.16am service from Pembroke Dock to Swansea.
W. G. Sumner/Geoff Wright

Tenby

A 1920s view of Tenby station taken from the station footbridge. Standing in the up platform is a stopping service from Pembroke Dock to Swansea. Notice also the large water tank on the down platform. The same view on 22 September 1993 shows Class 153 No 153312 on the 10.42am service to Pembroke Dock. Although the up platform building has been removed, the down side remains remarkably intact.
Real Photos/Geoff Wright

Pembroke Dock

The crew of '8100' class 2-6-2T No 8102 have a short break as it stands at Pembroke Dock in July 1950 with a through service to Paddington. Today there are no through services to Paddington but on 22 September 1993 Class 153 No 153312 waits with the 11.16am service for Swansea where it connects with the 12.32pm HST service to Paddington.
Real Photos/Geoff Wright

Pembroke Dock

'Manor' class 4-6-0 No 7804 *Baydon Manor* stands at Pembroke Dock on 24 August 1963 after arriving with the 10.55am service from Paddington, the 'Pembroke Coast Express'. Today the down platform is unused but the lovely stone entrance survives and can be seen to good effect on 22 September 1993 as Class 153 No 153312 waits with the 11.16am service to Swansea.
R. N. Joanes/Geoff Wright

Clarbeston Road

'Hall' class 4-6-0 No 5961 *Toynbee Hall* arrives at Clarbeston Road on 30 July 1956 with a service to Milford Haven. Clarbeston Road was the junction for the branches to Fishguard Harbour, Milford Haven and Neyland. The station has now been reduced to an unstaffed halt although both platforms are still in use. On 23 September 1993 Class 158 No 158832 arrives with the 2.29pm service to Milford Haven.
M. Hale/Geoff Wright

Haverfordwest

A view of Haverfordwest station looking east in 1959. The station was rebuilt by the Great Western in 1939 to give the layout seen here. Although both platforms are still in use, many services now arrive and depart from the up platform as in this shot of Class 158 No 158870 departing with the 11.47am service to Milford Haven on 23 September 1993.
R. G. H. Simpson/Geoff Wright

Milford Haven

Milford Haven station seen here on 13 December 1966. The station which is situated on a sharp curve contained a single platform and bay. The single track branch from Johnston was opened by the Great Western on 7 September 1863. In recent years the main station buildings have been removed and replaced by a single bus-type shelter and Portacabin. The basic facilities can be seen in this picture of Class 158 No 158870 as it waits to depart with the 12.34pm service to Swansea. Apart from the passenger services the branch sees a considerable amount of oil traffic from the large terminals at Milford Haven. *GW Trust/Geoff Wright*

Fishguard & Goodwick

Fishguard & Goodwick station was opened on 1 July 1899 and was the terminus of the branch from Clarbeston Road until the Harbour line was opened in 1906. The station was enlarged in 1907 when the track was doubled through to the Harbour. It is seen here on 31 August 1959 as a '5700' class 0-6-0PT No 4677 arrives with a stopping service to Clarbeston Road. The station was closed to passengers on 6 April 1964 but was briefly reopened during remodelling work at the harbour in the summer of 1982. The now derelict up platform is pictured here on 23 September 1993.
M. Hale/Geoff Wright

Gobowen

Gobowen and Oswestry are of course both situated in Shropshire but are included in this section because of their Cambrian connections. Gobowen stands on the ex-Great Western Shrewsbury-Chester line. From here a short branch connected with the Cambrian Railways at Oswestry. On 28 August 1952 a '2251' class 0-6-0 No 2244 stands in the bay platform with the 1.26pm service to Oswestry. The journey took just eight minutes!

Gobowen is still open and is remarkably intact, even the bay track is still *in situ*. The main station building however has been given over to commercial use. The old goods yard on the left is currently used by a local coal merchant. The station is now served by Regional Railways services between Chester and Shrewsbury.
B. Morrison/Author

Fishguard Harbour

A pair of Great Western 'City' class 4-4-0s stand at Fishguard Harbour with an up boat train to Paddington in the 1920s. As already mentioned, the Harbour station was opened on 30 August 1906 in connection with the new ferry service to Rosslare. In 1982 the station was reduced to just one platform and many of the sidings were removed. The station is now served by just two trains each weekday, a Regional Railways service to Cardiff and a through InterCity HST service to Paddington. On 23 September 1993 Class 158 No 158380 departs with the 1.50pm Cardiff service.
Real Photos/Geoff Wright

Chirk

The attractive station at Chirk seen here in the 1920s. The railway and Llangollen Canal rather spectacularly cross the Dee valley here on adjacent viaducts. The old buildings were removed during the 1960s and have now been replaced by a pair of rather attractive stone-built shelters. 15 September 1993. *Real Photos/Author*

Ruabon

Ruabon was once a very busy station, as apart from the main line services to Chester and Birkenhead it was also the junction station for services to Bala. Today it is an unstaffed halt, the station building being used by a design company. The station is seen here in better times as 'Castle' class 4-6-0 No 5095 *Barbury Castle* departs on 11 July 1962 with a through service from Birkenhead to Paddington. The run-down state of the station can be seen in this picture taken on 15 September 1993. *M. Pearson/Author*

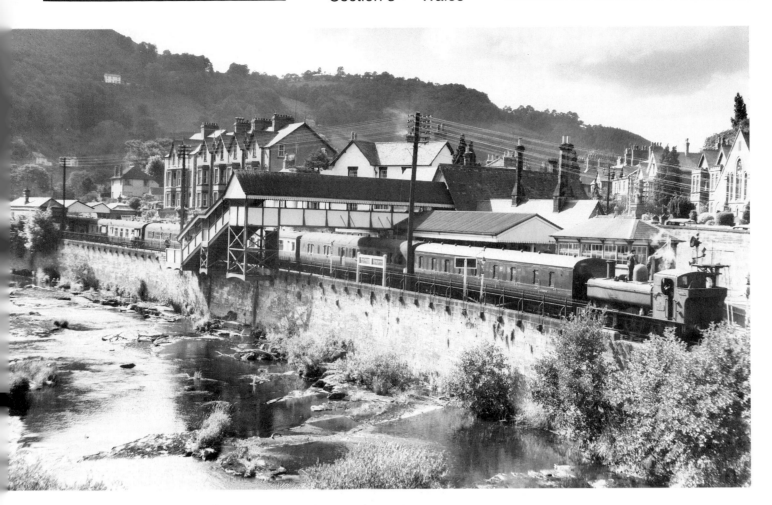

Llangollen

One of the more interesting stations on the now-closed branch from Ruabon to Bala Junction is at Llangollen. The station which is situated alongside the River Dee was closed to passenger traffic on 18 January 1965. Although the track was lifted the station buildings survived and in 1975 were taken over by the Flint & Deeside Railway Preservation Society (now the Llangollen Railway Society). By 1981 enough track had been relaid to run trains once again and since then the line has been extended through to Glyndyfrdwy a distance of 5½ miles, the eventual intention being to reinstate the track through to Corwen. The station at Llangollen is pictured here on 12 August 1960 and shows pannier 0-6-0 No 7442 on a service from Bala to Ruabon. On a very wet 15 September 1993 the excellent condition of the station can be clearly seen. *D. Cross/Author*

Bala
Bala station was situated on the Bala Junction-Blaenau Festiniog branch. On 3 March 1962 '5700' class 0-6-0PT No 3630 waits at Bala with a service to Bala Junction. The line and station were closed on 18 January 1965. On 26 September 1993 the Bala station site is in use as a municipal car park and industrial estate. The only reference points are the distant hills and the small stone building on the right which appears in both pictures. *A. Tyson/Peter Heath*

Llanuwchllyn
Against the dramatic backdrop of the Cambrian mountains a Standard Class 4 No 75006 departs from Llanuwchllyn in August 1964 with a morning service from Barmouth to Ruabon.

The station stood on the Bala Junction to Barmouth branch and was closed by BR on 18 January 1965 but on 14 August 1972 the station was taken over by the Bala Lake Railway. The station is now the terminus of the 4$\frac{1}{4}$-mile line. It is amazing just how little has changed in this picture taken on 26 September 1993. *E. J. S. Gadsden/ David Heath*

Wrexham General

Back to the main line once again and looking down from the overbridge at Wrexham General on 27 September 1958 'Castle' class No 5050 *Earl of St Germans* arrives with a service from Birmingham to Birkenhead. The main platforms here were staggered, the down platform being behind the photographer.

The scene has changed somewhat as Class 158 No 158843 approaches Wrexham on 15 September 1993 with the 11.4am service from Birmingham New Street to Chester.

T. Lewis/Author

243

Wrexham Central

At one time there were three stations at Wrexham; the ex-LNER station Wrexham Exchange was situated adjacent to the Great Western's General, being closed in the 1970s. The ex-Great Central/Cambrian joint station at Wrexham Central is still open. It is pictured here, looking east on 27 September 1958 as BR Class 2 No 78031 shunts some empty stock.

The ex-Cambrian branch closed on 10 September 1962 and today the Central station is the terminus for services from Bidston. The whole layout has now been reduced to a single line as seen on 15 September 1993. *T. Lewis/Author*

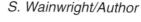

Chester

I have also included Chester in this section as it is the northern extent of this book and the terminus for services over the ex-Great Western main line to Birkenhead.

The ex-LNWR/GWR joint station at Chester was, and still is, an important interchange point for services from Birkenhead, Manchester, Crewe, Shrewsbury and North Wales. On 11 May 1963 'County' class 4-6-0 No 1000 *County of Middlesex* stands at platform 2 with the 2.45pm service to Birkenhead. Platforms 1 and 2 at Chester are now used for parcels services, although when I took this picture on 15 September 1993 platform 2 appeared to be out of use. Standing at the main parcels platform is the '08' station pilot, No 08585.
S. Wainwright/Author

Oswestry

Oswestry was the headquarters of the Cambrian Railways. It was here that the company had its offices and works. The station was closed on 7 November 1966 and today part of the site has been taken over by the Cambrian Railways Society. To illustrated the changing scene at Oswestry I have chosen this picture taken on 23 June 1956 which shows 'Manor' 4-6-0 No 7819 *Hinton Manor* shunting at Oswestry Goods. The yard closed on 6 December 1971 and looking down from the same footbridge on 15 September 1993 the site is now covered by a new road, a car park and a supermarket. The main reference point is the building on the right.
R. E. Vincent/ Author

Welshpool

'Manor' class 4-6-0 No 7823 *Hook Norton Manor* waits to depart from Welshpool with the down 'Cambrian Coast Express', the 11.10am ex-Paddington, on 31 March 1962. The station comprised three main platforms and a bay, and at one time boasted services to Aberystwyth, Pwllheli, Chester, Oswestry, Whitchurch and Shrewsbury, the latter being reached via Buttington junction. I must say I had quite a shock when I turned up on 14 September 1993 as the old station, although still standing, has been completely separated from the track by a new bypass. The new station can be seen under the enormous footbridge on the site of the old water tower and engine sidings. *Hugh Ballantyne/Author*

Montgomery
The morning Oswestry-Newtown pick-up freight hauled by ex-Great Western 'Dean Goods' 0-6-0 No 2538 leaves the small station at Montgomery on 4 April 1956. The station was closed on 14 June 1965; the signalbox lasted slightly longer, being closed on 20 July 1969. The station building is now in private ownership and is pictured here on 14 September 1993.
G. F. Bannister/Author

Newtown

The 'Manors' proved to be very good performers on Cambrian line services. On 2 September 1963 No 7822 *Foxcote Manor* stands at Newtown with a morning service to Aberystwyth. The town itself was quite important in years gone by as it was also the terminus of the Montgomeryshire Canal.

Newtown is one of several passing points on the route; the station, although basically intact, has now been downgraded to an unstaffed halt. Whilst waiting for an up service to arrive on 14 September 1993 a Class 31 No 31166 arrived with an inspection coach and promptly parked itself in the siding. This precluded taking a shot from the same position as the first picture (as it is not a good idea when the Chief Civil Engineer is around) so I have instead included this shot which shows the Class 31 parked in the down bay. *A. Muckley/Author*

Llanbrynmair
'Manor' class 4-6-0 No 7828 *Odney Manor* pulls into Llanbrynmair on 29 August 1963 with a service from Shrewsbury to Aberystwyth. The station is interesting as the down platform was actually bisected by a level crossing. This can be seen more clearly in the second picture. The station was closed on 14 June 1965 and today is in use as a private residence. It has been beautifully restored in chocolate and cream paint with lots of ex-GWR signs etc. *A. Muckley/David Heath*

Machynlleth

Machynlleth was an important centre on the Cambrian routes to Pwllheli and Aberystwyth. Apart from being a major passing point Machynlleth also had its own engine shed and carriage sidings. The fine station building can be seen behind '2251' class 0-6-0 No 2268 as it waits with the 4.16pm service from Shrewsbury to Aberystwyth on 31 August 1963.

The locomotive depot was closed to steam on 5 December 1966 but remained open for diesel servicing until 1990. Machynlleth maintains its importance as the 'Radio Signalling' centre for the ex-Cambrian lines. The new centre which was opened on 21 October 1988 controls all train movements between Sutton Bridge junction (Shrewsbury), Aberystwyth and Pwllheli. The station now has a rather run-down look as Class 153 units Nos 153334/5 arrive with the late running 2.4pm service from Birmingham New Street on 14 September 1993. The units will split here to form the 4.34pm Aberystwyth and 4.40pm Pwllheli services. *A. Muckley/Author*

Dovey Junction

Dovey Junction must be one of the most difficult stations to reach other than by train. It has no road access and being a considerable distance from the nearest road, to reach the station on foot means walking alongside or on the Aberystwyth line. The reason for this unusual state of affairs is of course that it was constructed solely as an interchange station for Aberystwyth and Pwllheli services.

It is seen here in 1958 as the signalman prepares to exchange tokens with the crew of 'Dukedog' 4-4-0 No 9012 which has just arrived from Aberystwyth. On the right a '4500' class 2-6-2T No 5541 has arrived with the connecting service from Pwllheli.

In recent years the station has seen some investment with a new shelter and platform lights. On 24 September 1993 Class 156 No 156413 arrives with the 2.4pm service from Birmingham to Aberystwyth and Pwllheli. The service has split at Machynlleth. *J. D. Edwards/David Heath*

Aberystwyth

'2251' class 0-6-0 No 2200 stands in the loco yard at Aberystwyth in May 1953. The engine shed which was a sub depot of Machynlleth closed to steam on 19 April 1965 but was subsequently used for the Vale of Rheidol locomotives and rolling stock. It is seen here on 14 September 1993; on the left is the Vale of Rheidol line to Devil's Bridge and on the right the single ex-Cambrian line to Dovey Junction. *Real Photos /Author*

Aberystwyth
Aberystwyth was once a busy station with through services to Carmarthen, Shrewsbury, Birmingham and London. One of the more important of these was the 'Cambrian Coast Express'. The Aberystwyth portion is seen here departing from platform 4 on 20 September 1965 headed by 'Manor' No 7812 *Erlestoke Manor*. Today the station has a very run-down look with BR services arriving and departing from what was platform 3. The old Carmarthen branch platform on the left is now used by the privately-owned Vale of Rheidol Railway. It seems that the whole of the remaining area may shortly be redeveloped with a new island platform being constructed for both services.
M. S. Welch/Author

Aberystwyth
Up until 1968 Vale of Rheidol services ran into their own station at Aberystwyth. This stood adjacent to the Great Western station, but from 20 May 1968 the VoR station was closed and the narrow gauge trains were diverted into the disused Carmarthen line bay at the main line station. Two of the three VoR engines Nos 7 *Owain Glyndwr* and 8 *Llywelyn* stand with their trains at Aberystwyth VoR in 1957. On 14 September 1993 the site of the old VoR station and trackbed is now a road but the small building on the right in both shots still stands and is nowadays used as a band hall.
J. D. Edwards/Author

Aberdovey

The 10.25am service from Pwllheli to Dovey Junction hauled by '4300' class 2-6-0 No 7335 pauses at Aberdovey on 12 July 1962. Note the ex-Cambrian signal on the right.

The passing loop was taken out some years ago but the down platform and goods bay are still *in situ* although overgrown. On the up side the station building remains almost intact and is now in use as a private residence. On Sunday 26 September 1993 Centro unit No 150125 and Regional Railways Class 156 No 156417 arrive with the 10.25am service from Pwllheli to Birmingham.
J. Scrace/David Heath

Barmouth

Against the magnificent backdrop of Cader Idris the 'Cambrian Radio Land Cruise' service, hauled by BR Standard Class 4 No 75052, approaches Barmouth on 15 August 1960.

Apart from the motive power there is little other change as on a misty 25 September 1993 a Class 156 No 156417 passes the same spot with the 2.4pm service from Birmingham New Street to Pwllheli. The 800yd-long wooden viaduct across the Mawddach Estuary was extensively renovated in the early 1980s. *P. Poulter/Peter Heath*

Barmouth

'Manor' class 4-6-0 No 7807 *Compton Manor* departs from Barmouth on 13 May 1955 with the 2.30pm service to Bala and Chester. This service ran via Barmouth junction and Dolgellau.

Both platforms are still in use but the footbridge has now been removed; the bay platform seen on the right in both pictures was closed in 1965. On 25 September 1993 Sprinter No 150202 departs with the 4.40pm service to Machynlleth. The signalbox which closed on 22 October 1988 is still *in situ* but at the time of writing was due for demolition. *R. Hewitt/Peter Heath*

List of Locations

A GWR publicity poster from the GWS collection.